OJIBWA NARRATIVES

Of Charles and Charlotte Kawbawgam
and Jacques LePique, 1893–1895

OJIBWA

Recorded with Notes by Homer H. Kidder

The John M. Longyear Research Library
Marquette County Historical Society

NARRATIVES

Of Charles and Charlotte Kawbawgam
and Jacques LePique, 1893–1895

Edited by Arthur P. Bourgeois

Wayne State University Press

Detroit

GREAT LAKES BOOKS

A complete listing of the books in this series can be
found at the back of this volume.

Philip P. Mason, Editor
Department of History, Wayne State University
Dr. Charles K. Hyde, Associate Editor
Department of History, Wayne State University

Copyright © 1994 by Wayne State University Press, Detroit,
Michigan 48202. All rights are reserved. No part of this book may be
reproduced without formal permission.
Manufactured in the United States of America.
99 98 97 96 95 94   5 4 3 2 1
Library of Congress Cataloging-in-Publication Data
Kawbawgam, Charles, d. 1902.
Ojibwa narratives of Charles and Charlotte Kawbawgam and Jacques
LePique, 1893-1895 / recorded, with notes, by Homer H. Kidder ;
edited by Arthur P. Bourgeois.
   p.   cm.—(Great Lakes books)
Includes bibliographical references.
ISBN 0-8143-2514-9 (alk. paper).—ISBN 0-8143-2515-7 (pbk. : alk. paper)
1. Ojibwa Indians—Legends. 2. Ojibwa Indians—History.
I. Kawbawgam, Charlotte, ca. 1831-1904. II. LePique, Jacques.
III. Kidder, Homer H. (Homer Huntington), 1874-1950. IV. Bourgeois,
Arthur P. (Arthur Paul), 1940-   V. Title. VI. Series.
E99.C6K38   1994
973'.04973—dc20   93-32783

Designer: Mary Krzewinski

Grateful acknowledgment is made to the American Philosophical Society in Philadelphia for permission to use and publish Homer H. Kidder's manuscript. The original,
323-page handwritten manuscript, is part of the APS collection.

Contents

ACKNOWLEDGMENTS 9   EDITOR'S INTRODUCTION 11   INTRODUCTORY NOTE 21

Nanabozho (Kawbawgam) *25*
Kawbawgam's Remarks on Nanabozho *30*
How Nanabozho Came to Have a Wolf Companion (Jacques LePique) *32*
Nanabozho in Time of Famine (Kawbawgam) *33*
The Diver (Kawbawgam) *36*

Nanabozho Plays at Being Dead (Kawbawgam) *37*
The Lost War Party (Kawbawgam) *38*
Thunderbirds and the Medicine Root (Kawbawgam) *40*
The Mishi Ginabig and the Thunderbirds (Kawbawgam) *42*
Mishi Ginabig in Lake Michigamme (Jacques LePique) *43*

Water Spirits in Sable Lake (Jacques LePique) *45*
The Curing of I-que-wa-gun (Kawbawgam) *48*
The Great Turtle (Kawbawgam) *51*
The Girl and the Midéwug (Jacques LePique) *52*
The Midéwiwin (Kawbawgam) *55*

CONTENTS

The Jessakkiwin and the Midé (Kaw-
  bawgam) *57*
The Jessakkiwin (Kawbawgam) *59*
The Cedar Knife (Jacques LePique) *61*
Paying the Devil (Jacques LePique) *65*
Fasting and Medicine Songs (Jacques
  LePique) *67*

Iron Maker (Jacques LePique) *69*
Note on Iron Maker *70*
Kwasind (Jacques LePique) *71*
Nibawnawbé (Homer H. Kidder) *74*
A Famine and How a Medicine Man
  Saved the People (Kawbawgam) *79*

Fragment of a Medicine Story (Jacques
  LePique) *81*
The Snow Rabbit and the North Wind
  (Homer H. Kidder) *83*
The Man Who Died Three Times
  (Jacques LePique) *84*
The Man from the World Above
  (Jacques LePique) *85*
The Robin (Jacques LePique) *89*

The Whippoorwill (Charlotte Kaw-
  bawgam) *90*
The Sister's Ghost (Charlotte Kaw-
  bawgam) *91*
The Beast Men (Jacques LePique) *92*
The Great Skunk (Kawbawgam) *96*
The Great Bear of the West (Kaw-
  bawgam) *97*

The Great Skunk and the Great Bear of
  the West (Homer H. Kidder) *101*
Wampum Hair (Jacques LePique) *102*
The Girls and the Porcupine (Kawbawgam) *108*

Contents

Chickadee Boy (Kawbawgam) *109*

The League of the Four Upper Algonquian Nations (Kawbawgam) *112*

Fight with the Iroquois (Kawbawgam) *114*

Two Stories of Sauks Head (Jacques
LePique and Charlotte Kawbawgam) *116*

Sauks at Portage Entry (Jacques
LePique) *122*

Some Ojibwa History (Kaw-
bawgam) *124*

Wyagaw (Kawbawgam) *126*

Our Brother-in-Law's Adventures (Kawbawgam) *129*

Aitkin and the Ojibwa (Jacques
LePique) *131*

The Story of a Half-breed (Jacques
LePique) *134*

Major Rains (Kawbawgam) *138*

Jacques LePique's Reminiscences, Preliminary Note (Homer H.
Kidder) *139*

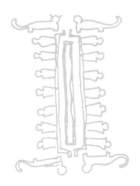

Reminiscences of Jacques LePique—A
Journey to the Arctic (Jacques
LePique) *141*

Adventures on the Prairie (about 1833)
A Massacre by the Sioux (Jacques
LePique) *142*

Jacques' Life at the Sault and on Lake Superior (Jacques LePique) *144*

Overland Trails (Kawbawgam and
Jacques LePique) *152*

Some Ojibwa Place Names (Kawbawgam and Jacques LePique) *154*

CONTENTS

Ojibwa Names of the Twelve Moons or
   Months of the Year (Kawbawgam and
   Jacques LePique) *158*
Notes On Kawbawgam (Homer H.
   Kidder) *159*

APPENDIX 161   BIBLIOGRAPHY 163

Acknowledgments

It is a pleasure to thank the people and institutions who made the publication of this work possible. Special thanks are due to Dr. Bernard C. Peters for bringing this manuscript to my attention and to James Carter, William Trevarrow, Kathy Peters, and Linda Panian of the Marquette County Historical Society for their kind assistance. The Marquette County Historical Society also provided the photos that appear in this book.

I extend deepest thanks to my secretary, Susan Inman, for arduous hours of transcription and numerous suggestions in the editing of this work. Gratitude is likewise due to Burt Kinister and Jonathan Mantel for their relief shifts in the initial transcription and to Mary Sallander for pursuit of inter-library loan materials. I am most grateful for the encouragement of my father, Paul A. Bourgeois, to whom this editorial work is dedicated. Lastly, it is through the kindness of the American Philosophical Society of Philadelphia that permission has been received to publish the H. H. Kidder manuscript.

Arthur P. Bourgeois

Editor's Introduction

We live immersed in stories, the narratives that we tell or hear told, stories that we imagine, sometimes semi-consciously recounting our past actions, anticipating future outcome or situating ourselves at the intersection of stories not yet completed. Narratives can be viewed as a way of knowing or remembering, and as a means of shaping or patterning emotions and experiences into something whole and meaningful. When told, these storied events become larger than ordinary life, liberating us from the emphasis on the daily toil. Stories show us who we are, bridge commonalities of experience, and instill a sense of belonging when delivered in keeping with audience expectations. Narratives that tell of origins, why the world is the way it is, why we do as we do, and what we are supposed to do constitute a particular kind of story. Why certain of these stories are accepted and retained and why some aspects are repressed from one version to another begs broader consideration. Changes are made in their repeating and yet common patterns exist that are distinctive of individual regions and ethnicity. Social organization, belief systems, and personality patterns are all reflected within them but so too are the contradictions and ambiguities of the human condition.

The life ways of Native Americans have attracted widespread interest for over three centuries, beginning with the writings of European missionaries and early travelers to North America. During the nineteenth century, narratives of the Ojibwas in particular received special attention through the work of Henry Rowe Schoolcraft, and thereby entered American literature through Longfellow's epic poem "Hiawatha." To suit the literary tastes of that era, the writings transformed the original narratives almost beyond recognition. Subsequent published studies of Ojibwa folklore from north or east of Lake Superior (Skinner, Jones, Laidlaw, Radin, Landes, Morriseau, and Johnston), Michigan (Kohl, Blackbird, Kinietz), Minnesota (de Jong and Coleman) and Wisconsin (Barnouw) greatly expand the corpus of known tales, although most are difficult to obtain or are hidden amid more esoteric studies. Portions of the above and others have been anthologized by A. F. Chamberlain and A. Helbig and are listed in an extensive bibliography published by C. Vecsey. With the exception of C. Vecsey's recent publication, no reference has been given to the body of material collected by H. H. Kidder.

The following narratives derive from the Ojibwa ethnic group (also termed Chippewa by the United States Government or Anishnabeg as they call themselves), a people who expanded both to the southeast and westward from a base point at Sault Sainte Marie in the late seventeenth through nineteenth centuries. Their settlements were originally made up of small autonomous bands scattered throughout an extensive area largely to the north of Lakes Superior and Huron, engaged in a hunting-fishing-gathering type of economy. Only the southernmost units gardened corn, beans and squash, gathered maple sugar and wild rice, and developed a slightly more elaborate sociopolitical organization. Seasonal shifting in search of wild foods necessitated a seminomadic way of life generally based in a summer fishing village yet largely remaining within a fifty-mile radius. For example, during winter months, the Ojibwa dispersed as individual families in order to hunt deer or small game animals. In March a number of families would gather in a sugar bush camp for tapping and processing maple sap to be used throughout the year as seasoning, candy, and a refreshing drink when mixed with water.

Their more stationary dwelling consisted of an elliptical dome-shaped structure made of a pole frame covered with rolls of birchbark and cattail matting. The largest examples could house several families. The interior sheltered woven cedarbark mats, woven bags, a variety of birchbark containers, carved wooden bowls, ladles, bow and arrows, snowshoes, cradleboard, fish lures, nets, and line, and perhaps lacrosse racquets, flute, drum, and (rarely) sculptured imagery in human and animal form. Tanned hide clothing, medicine bag, and knife sheath occasionally featured dyed porcupine quillwork, or later, glass bead decoration arranged in floral designs, while patterns in silk applique were sparingly applied toward the end of the eighteenth century.

Social life centered on visiting between relatives and friends either in the process of daily labor or before and after feasts, ceremonials, and social dances. Although aboriginal Ojibwa were egalitarian and classless, there were people of prestige who achieved special acknowlegment as orators, religious leaders, or warriors. As part of each individual's identity, everyone belonged to a designated clan, with marriage required into a different clan (although children belonged to the clan of their father). Certain clans, moreover, were linked as phratries providing one another with special hospitality and mutual assistance.

Editor's Introduction

Ojibwa religious life was largely personal—directed to one's guardian spirit acquired in a vision quest. Of major importance were a host of spirits (*manito*) that inhabited the natural world, some dwelling in the sky, some on earth, and others underground or underwater. Of major importance were the four winds, the thunderbird, the sun, and a paramount presiding spirit (*kitchi manito*), while malevolent water monsters, cannibalistic giants, ghosts, and witches were greatly feared. Prayers, together with offerings of tobacco and food, honored or placated these forces. Smoking tobacco constituted the initial rite for all religious and ceremonial occasions as well as for establishing social relationships. Individuals of distinct supernatural power acquired through a vision quest and specialized training, known in the literature as shamans, were both feared and respected. Several varieties of shamanistic performance are noted among the Ojibwa: the conjuror (jessakid), who employed the shaking-tent technique mainly for curing but also to locate lost persons or articles; the sucking doctor, who removed disease from a patient by sucking it out through a bone tube; and the *wabano,* a sorcerer who furnished hunting and love charms and demonstrated power through acts of superhuman physical abilities. In addition, the Medicine Lodge Society (*midéwiwin*), a curative association to which membership was obtained by preliminary instruction, payment of considerable fees, and formal initiation, had priests (*midé*) who drove out sickness by "shooting" a shell into the candidate's body. Considerable overlapping between these functions is evident with conjurors and sucking doctors also functioning as *midé* priests and no two sorcerers operating exactly the same.

During the long winter months, folktales handed down for many generations were told by elders around the fire not only to entertain but to affirm belonging and to teach ethnical precepts. Their narration was a dignified matter usually accompanied by a gift and preceeded by a feast. Yet considerable scope was given to the story-teller's imagination, allowing dramatized narration, and incorporation of new material. The role of the masterful story-teller was itself legendary as one who knew hundreds of marvellous stories that could make people laugh and cry, be fearful or ponder their significance. But to be exceptionally facile with speech was also to invite envy and be accused of "knowing too much."

The stories narrated by Charles Kawbawgam, his wife Charlotte, and brother-in-law, Jacques LePique between 1893 and 1895 are not timeless. They reflect a nostalgic view to this earlier period when the heart of Ojibwa seminomadic culture remained intact—a time when the fur trade together with seasonal roving, traditional transportation, and indigenous practices of child rearing, religious thought, art, and music permeated daily life. After the 1830's, the fur trade which had endured for two hundred years came upon hard times, with the gradual dwindling of furred and large game animals and eventual collapse of the world fur market. Increasing economic and psychological dependence upon traders for goods, clothing, and winter foodstuffs, political advice and paternal leadership left inhabitants on the south shore of Lake Superior particularly vulnerable. Although exploitation was tempered by missionaries like Frederick Baraga and Leonard H. Wheeler, who strove to develop an agrarian economy among the Ojibwa, acculturation soon included dressing like whites, dwelling in log buildings, and attending white churches and schools. In 1836 and again in 1842, representatives of the Lake Superior Ojibwa sold their hunting grounds in the treaties of Washington and LaPointe in return for payoffs to traders and half bloods, twenty-five year annuity schedules, and the right to remain temporarily in the ceded regions subject to the pleasure of the United States president. By 1845, white developers were prying everywhere, soon followed by the invasion of miners, lumbermen, farmers, and town builders. Ojibwa participation was reduced to supplying white communities with fish and fuel and other marginal activities. Allotted land reserves, too small to maintain a traditional hunting-gathering-fishing economy, led to increasing poverty and dependence upon local and federal government largess.

In the early 1890's, when the following narratives were recorded, commerce on Lake Superior had reached an all time high, with the opening of the Poe locks at Sault Ste. Marie. A network of railways not only connected iron ore mines to sophisticated loading docks but linked the Upper Peninsula to major midwest centers. By 1890, Marquette had become a city with a population of ten thousand, a newly operating hydroelectric power plant, and a variety of industries including a bottling works, a sizeable foundry that manufactured gas engines, and brownstone quarries annually shipping a hundred thousand cubic feet of building stone. Also during this period, a Marquette Branch of the Michigan State Prison opened, Peter White Public Library was founded, and negotiations were underway for establishment of a Normal School which later became Northern Michigan University. In brief, the region, although still largely forested, was no longer hinterland. Each of the three storytellers included here had spent most of five decades living near or in the burgeoning white communities. This experience must have affected their attitudes, recollections, and the selection of narratives they related to Kidder.

Charles Kawbawgam ("Charlie Bawgam") was of the Bosinasse or Echo-maker-Crane totemic clan of Sault Ste. Marie which claimed prominence over other Ojibwa clans by hereditary right. His father was Black Cloud (Mukcawday mawquot or Muk-Ku-day-wuk-kwud according

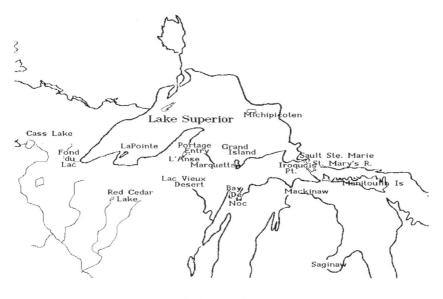

Lake Superior.

to Kidder)—a name cited in the treaties of 1820 and 1836 as a chief of the second class. His stepfather was Shaweno Kewainze, also known as Ka-ga-qua-dung, the head chief of the Sault Ojibwa in 1855 and the last prominent chief to make his home at the rapids. His mother was Charlotte Sare of Scottish-Indian descent. Kawbawgam's true Ojibwa name was Nawaquay-geezhik (Noon Day), a name cited as a headman at the Sault in the Treaties of 1855. Kawbawgam is a nickname. Kawbawgam lived at Sault Ste. Marie, met Charlotte there, and came to the Marquette region with Robert Graveraet around 1848. Kawbawgam's chieftainship derived from his claimed succession to Madosh (Kawgayosh), a head-chief recognized by the U.S. Government. The fame of his lineage together with his bearing and advanced age reinforced local acclaim to this otherwise landless chief. The Carp River group merged periodically with that on Grand Island as described in the 1832 Journal of Lieutenant James Allen while the Treaty of 1836 recognized Kaug Wyanais as second class chief at "Carp River west of Grand Island" and "Ashegons, Kinuwais, Misquaonaby, and Mongons" as headmen from the "Carp and Chocolate [Chocolay] Rivers." This was, as C. Fred Rydholm noted, but one segment of the larger Noquet band of the bear totemic clan that

15

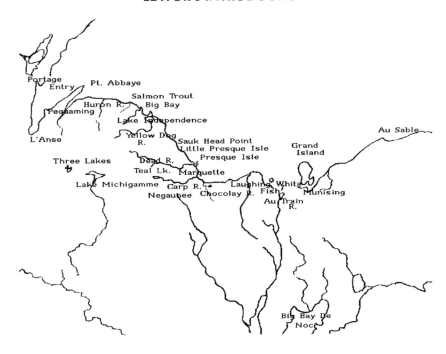

South shore of Lake Superior, central region.

traditionally summered along the southern shore of Lake Superior east of Keweenaw and wintered at Bay de Noc.

Kawbawgam remained a periodic celebrity in Independence Day parades in Marquette at the turn of the century. Ralph D. Williams, in his book *The Honorable Peter White*, mentions Kawbawgam's arrest (and subsequent acquittal) in old age by a game warden for setting a sucker net in a stream. Kawbawgam and his family received local support from Peter White and Alfred Kidder who also built a cabin for them at Presque Isle. Kawbawgam died at St. Mary's Hospital in Marquette on December 28, 1902. According to his obituary, he had been a practicing Roman Catholic. Funeral services were held at St. Peter's Cathedral and a splendid funerary cortege led to his burial site at Presque Isle.

Kawbawgam's wife, Charlotte (in Ojibwa, Minwash, Sailing with the Wind), was the daughter of Susan, the second wife of Matji-gijig (Bad Day)—commonly rendered in local history as Marje-gesick. She is said to have been born around 1831. Charlotte stated at a judicial inquest that she and Charles were married at Sault Ste. Marie by a Roman Catholic

16

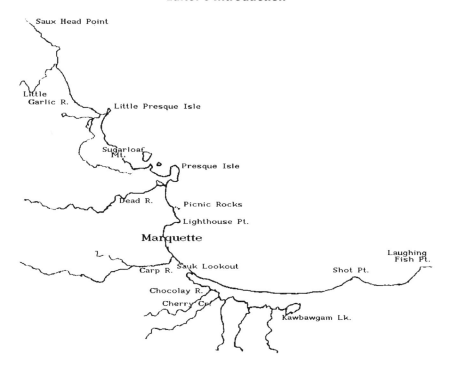

Saux Head Point

Little
Garlic R.

Little Presque Isle

Sugarloaf
Mt.

Presque Isle

Dead R.

Picnic Rocks

Lighthouse Pt.

Mar quette

Laughing
Fish Pt.

Carp R. Sauk Lookout

Shot Pt.

Chocolay R.

Cherry Cr.

Kawbawgam Lk.

Marquette area.

priest. Charlotte had two children who died at birth or in infancy, and later the couple adopted a son and daughter, Fred and Charlotte Codotte. Kawbawgam and his wife settled north of the mouth of the Carp River in a log house known to the first white settlers as "Bawgam House" but also lived for a time at Kawbawgam Lake and along Cherry Creek, Light House Point, upper Chocolay River, and on Presque Isle. Charlotte inherited a certificate of interest in the Jackson Mining Company deriving from her father's role in the discovery of iron ore in May of 1846 in the Negaunee Range but little came of this despite prolonged litigation in state courts. Blind in her old age, Charlotte died in 1904 and was buried next to her husband. A large boulder and inscription mark this well-known site at Marquette on Presque Isle.

Details regarding the life and forebear of Jacques LePique (his true name was Francis Nolin) are aptly told in several of the narratives and commentaries by Kidder. LePique was the son of Louis Nolin, a mixed

17

blood who clerked for the American Fur Company at Grand Island. He was called Jacques or Jaque LePique by the Canadian French, meaning the Jack of Spades or the Joker. To many Americans his name was further corrupted to Jack LePete.

Homer Huntington Kidder, the collector of these narratives, was born in Marquette in 1874, oldest son of Alfred and Kate Dalliba Kidder and brother of noted archaeologist Alfred Vincent Kidder. Upon entering Harvard University, Homer was forced by illness to leave college and spent two years with his father in Marquette and his summers at the Huron Mountain Club. During this period he collected Ojibwa folk narratives from Jacques LePique, Charles Kawbawgam and his wife, and sculpted a bust of Kawbawgam. He graduated from Harvard in 1899 and taught English composition as a teaching assistant at both Harvard and Radcliffe. In 1904, he joined the excavation staff of Rafael Pumpelly, Sr., at Merv in the Russian Turkistan and made a caravan journey across Russian Asia to Kashgar in China. He was variously employed in Minnesota on the newspaper staff of *The Bellman,* Minneapolis, and Brown-Burt Lumber Company, and then as an apple rancher on the Columbia River in Washington. During the first World War he returned to Europe as an ambulance driver for the Red Cross and conducted relief trains to Austria and the Balkan countries as a Red Cross major. Later he studied physical anthropology in Zurich and undertook archaeological research of the Dordogne cave deposits in central France for which he was awarded the Legion of Honor. With the German occupation in 1940, he moved to Nice where he, together with his second wife, Lilia Moreno, engaged in war relief activities. He suffered a stroke after settling in Berkeley, California, and last visited the Upper Peninsula of Michigan as a semi-invalid in 1949 seeking information pertaining to his collection of Ojibwa folktales. He died in Cambridge on December 5, 1950.

Ojibwa oral traditions of the mythic personage Nanabozho claimed primary importance in the winter evening recital of stories about the various manitos. The first four tales and an extended commentary as told by Kawbawgam are devoted to this central character of Ojibwa narrative. Nanabozho (variously termed Manabozho, Menabozho, Nenawbozho, Wenebojo, Manabush and Nanabush among diverse bands of the Ojibwa and their Algonkian-speaking neighbors) was viewed as a superhuman, a large white rabbit, creator and culture-hero, malicious prankster, and clown. He could take on many forms in his interaction with various manitos and humans, destroy monsters, protect against disease, ward off storms or famine, or prepare the way to the afterlife. Yet Nanabush's world, and that of traditional Ojibwa thought, was one where powers of the heavens such as thunderbirds were forever at war with powers beneath, namely, the horned snakes and their albino animal allies. Upon the earth's surface curiously shaped rocks, forceful springs, and isolated lakes were the abode of powerful beings and coastal rocky outcrops hid miniature people who could pass through stone; to say nothing about cannibal giants brought by frigid north winds.

The following tales bring alive this world where some people and beings assuredly have more powers that do others, where visible forms can be very deceptive, and transformations from human form to animal or its reverse are definite possibilities. Relevant evidence of these epic struggles is everywhere: in the large boulders scattered here and there, peculiarities of a rocky shoreline, coloration or anatomical features of animals and birds, and in general how they came to be the way they are. Still other narratives refer to Ojibwa ritual practice like the puberty fast and dream quest, conjuring by means of the "shaking tent," the role of powerful shamans, and the Midéwiwin grand medicine society. Armed conflicts with the Iroquois, Sauk, and Fox and alliances with the Ottawa, Potawatomi, and Menominee are equally detailed, not with the remoteness of an ethnologist or historian, but rather from within the living tradition.

Traditional conventions of story telling are found in LePique's suggestion that Kidder take pipe and tobacco to Presque Isle to present to Kawbawgam when arrangements were first made to record these stories; similarly the remark that Kawbawgam always smoked in silence between stories (p. 75, n. 61). Kidder equally mentions the pantomimes of Kawbawgam which set companions in an uproar (p. 35, n. 12) and other occasions of laughter (p. 130, n. 100). Noticeably absent from this collection are examples of Ojibwa bawdy and sexual humor which likely reflect either Christian influenced propriety or the relationship of the informants to the youthful and proper son of their mutual benefactor. Equally missing are a complete cycle of Nanabozho stories, and women's stories such as those that treat the foolish sisters Matchikwewis and Oshkikwe.

Aside from the manuscript itself, there is little to inform the reader regarding the manner in which the narratives were told by these three people and accurately recorded by a fourth. As stated by Kidder, they were told in Ojibwa, translated by LePique who spoke heavily accented English and eventually written down in their present form. This would not have been the first time LePique had heard these stories and he likely knew most of them as well as Kawbawgam. What he translated was probably a combination of what was said on that occasion and what LePique knew. Kidder also provides more than one version to two of the narratives, which gives evidence that he too reworked the material, cutting out redundancy and strengthening dramatic effect. It is likely that

EDITOR'S INTRODUCTION

Kidder's later awareness of deficiences of his transcription comes at a time when ethnologists Frances Densmore, Ruth Landes, and William Jones were conducting Ojibwa field research; this manuscript remained unpublished during his lifetime.

The 323-page, handwritten manuscript by Kidder is presently in the collection of the American Philosophical Society, Philadelphia (Freeman Guide 101 & 2506; APS Film 1394). Editing of this manuscript has entailed rearrangement of the order of presentation so that similar subjects are grouped together. Narratives treating Nanabozho and other supernatural beings and related institutions (pp. 25–88) are followed by incidental tales (pp. 89–111) which in turn are succeeded by historical accounts (pp. 112–151). Lastly, information regarding trails, place names, and months of the year are listed followed by a general bibliography. A listing of the original order of narratives and supplementary materials is to be found in the appendix. Kidder's footnotes have been included and are supplemented by those of the editor; these are designated as *Editor's Note* or placed between brackets within the text. Kidder's interjections appear within parentheses. The three narratives contained in H. H. Kidder's notes, "How Nanabozho Came to Have a Wolf Companion," "The Snow Rabbit and the North Wind" and "The Diver," collected from the same informants, are here incorporated into the text. As two versions of "Nibawnawbé" and "Two Stories of Sauks Head" appear in the original manuscript, both are included here. Because of the pejorative connotation of the term "halfbreed," the title of the original manuscript, "Ojibwa Myths and Halfbreed Tales," has been changed.

An effort has been made to retain Kidder's spellings of proper names, Ojibwa words and phrases although they may differ from that given by contemporary writers. Thus Kidder's Mishi Bizi, Mishi Ginabig and kinnikinick are retained rather than rendering them as Mishibiji, Mishiginebig, and kinnikinnik. Inconsistencies in punctuation and spelling, for example Chisakiwin, Tchessakiwin and Jessakkiwin are regularized as Jessakkiwin, although his use of Jessakkiwin and Jessakid have been retained. Dr. John D. Nichols, professor of native studies at the University of Manitoba, Winnipeg, has served as editorial consultant.

Introductory Note

These traditional tales were related to me near Marquette, Michigan on the south shore of Lake Superior, in the summers of 1893–1895, by a group of three persons, the Ojibwa chief, Charles Kawbawgam,[1] his Ojibwa wife, Charlotte,[2] and the latter's half-breed brother-in-law, Jacques LePique.[3] Only four tales were given me by Charlotte, but the collection comprises all of the tales known to the two men, or at least all that they said [they] could recall.

My informants were all of such advanced age that in their youth Lake Superior was still a wilderness without a town, and the Ojibwas, though undoubtedly much influenced by generations of contact with missionaries, traders, and voyagers, were still comparatively primitive, even at the eastern end of the lake, the section of the tribe from which all my informants sprang.

Kawbawgam grew up at the Sault Ste. Marie where he was born, and afterwards lived for some fifty years along the eastern half of the south shore of Lake Superior, particularly in the neighborhood of Iron Bay (Marquette) which was the native section of his wife. The Kawbawgams were comparatively sedentary, spoke no language but their own, and to the end of their days, after the country was settled by white people, remained very Indian and Ojibwa in their manner of living and thinking. Kawbawgam was a pronounced conservative and lamented the transformations which had come over his country and the life of the Indians. The stories he gave me, even those that recite incidents in his own

---

[1] Kawbawgam's original name was Nawaquay-geezhik (Noon Day). See note on his parentage, etc.[p. 159]. He had a strain of Scotch blood, through his mother, Charlotte Sare, a half-breed.

[2] The daughter of Matji-gijig, an Ojibwa Chief of the Eastern South Shore, she was born at Pine River and her Ojibwa name means "Sailing with the wind."

[3] His real name was Francis Nolin.

Homer Huntington Kidder, ca. 1899.

experience, are uniformly concerned with the ancient lore of his people, in which he retained unquestioning faith. They represent a stage of Ojibwa culture that has now quite disappeared in that part of the tribe. His wife was even less influenced by American life than he.

Jacques LePique, on the other hand, though sprung of Ojibwa half-breed parentage from the Sault, was born in the remote Cree Country, where he died, and though after the age of fourteen he lived most of his long life in the same region with the Kawbawgams, he was far less settled, moving about a good deal sometimes to the most distant parts of the Ojibwa country, and indeed travelled far beyond the range of the tribe. He was a half-breed, he spoke fluent English and Canadian French besides Cree and Ojibwa; he remained more or less a wanderer all his days. He gave me a number of primitive tales, for he had grown up among the Indians and was steeped in their lore; but in addition, he gave me a good many stories that reflect the life of the half-breeds and voyageurs of Lake Superior. These I call half-breed tales. In some respects, they seem to me hardly less interesting than the old Ojibwa myths, and they too represent a phase of culture which has all but disappeared from the Upper Lakes.

The stories related in Ojibwa by Charlotte and Kawbawgam, at their house at Presque Isle, were interpreted for me by Jacques LePique, and I took them down with a pencil as he slowly translated. His English was that of the Canadian French, marked by an accent but fluent and sometimes surprisingly adequate. I have not tried to reproduce the peculiarities of his dialect but have tried to express his thoughts as accurately as I could in readable English. It has proved anything but an easy task and I am far from being satisfied with the result. The lore of any folk should, if possible, be recorded in their own language. I am well aware that the use of an interpreter is a makeshift. Still I have felt it was worthwhile to record these tales as carefully interpreted. In the case of such as have been recorded, the versions in this collection may present local variations of interest.

My informants realized that their ancestral lore was passing from the memories of their people, and they gave me the tales with the understanding that these should be preserved in writing if not in print. I regret that other concerns have so long delayed the completion of this task.

Paris, February 1, 1910

Nanabozho

Kawbawgam

Nanabozho had a young wolf whom he called his nephew.[4] They lived on the shore of a lake and, when it froze over, he told the wolf that he must never cross it on the ice.

"Early or late," said he, "always go around this lake, for at the bottom are spirits who are my enemies and, if they should catch you on the ice, they would kill you."

But once, coming home late from hunting, the wolf struck across the lake. In the middle, the ice went to pieces beneath him, broken by the spirits, and the wolf was drowned.

Then Nanabozho gave a long cry and mourned aloud. All through the winter and the spring, he would go about the lake moaning for his nephew, seeking in his mind a plan to be revenged. He could not rest till revenged.

He knew that in the summer, on the hottest days, the spirits rose from the bottom of the lake to the surface, and he found a beach where they used to sleep in the sun. There, on a hot day, he changed himself into a pine stub, with the stoutest roots, and there he waited.

By and by, as the sun got higher, the spirits began to look out from the water, one after another, frogs, toads, lizards, and snakes, also bears, skunks, beavers and others, for although they were spirits, they came to the top in the shapes of animals. The last to come was in the form of a snow white panther, Mishi Bizi, the chief of the water spirits. He looked all about and, seeing the pine stub, said to the others: "Look at that stub. What do you think of it?"

---

[4] How Nanabozho came to have a wolf is told in a version of this story related to my father in the [eighteen] sixties by Jacques LePique [see p. 32].

The spirits answered: "We have never seen it before. It may be Nanabozho."[5]

The chief sent a *Mishi Ginabig,* the great serpent, on shore to try the stub. He was one of the strongest among them. He had immense antlers and he was as big as the largest pines. He coiled himself around the stub and hugged it with all his might, but Nanabozho did not make a sound.

The Mishi Ginabig said: "This is not Nanabozho." But the chief sent a still more powerful spirit, a yellow bear, who went at the stub and tore it with his claws till Nanabozho had to hold his breath to keep from howling. He would not cry out because his heart was set on revenge. He had a terrible will for revenge.

The yellow bear said: "No, no! This is not Nanabozho." Still the chief was not satisfied. He sent the most powerful spirit of them all, a monstrous red bear. Nothing could stand before him, rocks or trees. He rushed at the stub again and again, being sure that if it was Nanabozho he could knock it down but the roots were so strong that he could not budge it. So the red bear gave up too. He said: "This cannot be Nanabozho."

All this time the spirits had been floating in the water, but now they believed they were safe and came out on the beach. There they lay in a ring around the white panther and one by one, they fell asleep. Then Nanabozho took his own shape and strung his bow. Jumping over the spirits, he shot an arrow into the body of Mishi Bizi, near the heart. The panther roared and Nanabozho leaped over the others into the woods, while the spirits dove into the lake.

Nanabozho believed that he had killed his enemy and avenged the wolf. His heart was glad.

One day, meeting Mishi Bizi's grandmother, the Frog Woman, he saw that she had been crying. He said: "What's the matter?" He supposed it was the death of Mishi Bizi that made her cry. She answered: "My grandson was shot by Nanabozho and the arrow is still in him. I am doctoring him. If it hadn't been for me, he would have died." So Nanabozho knew that Mishi Bizi was still alive.

The old woman was packing a load of basswood bark and Nanabozho asked her what she was going to do with it.

She answered: "I am going to make a string and run it through the woods, tied on the trees, so that we can see if Nanabozho touches it somewhere."

---

[5] At this point Kawbawgam says: "Nanabozho must have had more power than the spirits for they could not tell whether it was Nanabozho or not."

Charles Kawbawgam, ca. 1880.

"But don't you suppose," said he, "that Nanabozho would see your string and would keep from touching it?"

"Maybe you are Nanabozho yourself," said the Frog Woman.

"Oh, no! I'm not Nanabozho," said he. "I am only telling you what I would do if I were Nanabozho. But what happens if Nanabozho does touch the string?"

"Why then, perhaps I could tell where he is," said the Frog Woman.

"We are going to send a shower of rocks, so that Nanabozho will be killed."

"You must think Nanabozho is a fool," said he. "Couldn't he hide somewhere till the stones stopped falling?"

The old woman then felt pretty sure she was talking with Nanabozho, but he laughed and said: "No, no. I never saw this Nanabozho. I'm just saying what I'd do if I were Nanabozho."

Next day he met her again and asked her when the rocks were going to fall. She answered: "Tomorrow."

So Nanabozho piled trees across a narrow ravine, and when the shower of rocks began, he went underneath and sat there till it was over. Before that, there were no great rocks on the earth. It was then that they fell where we see them today, such as the Pictured Rocks, Sugar Loaf, the Gull Rock, and the rest.

When the spirits found that Nanabozho was not killed by the rain of rocks, they sent a terrible winter, hoping to freeze him to death. This was the first winter. Snow covered all the earth. But Nanabozho made snow shoes, the first ever made. He could run on the snow, while deer and other animals were stuck in drifts. So he had plenty of game, and when the spirits sent chickadees to see if he was still alive, he pelted them with balls of fat.

When the winter was over, Nanabozho met the Frog Woman once more and asked her what was going to happen. She said: "The spirits are going to flood the world, and Nanabozho will be drowned."

The old woman was on her way to a cave where the spirits lived under the lake. She told him that she went there to doctor her grandson every evening when the door of the cave opened. Nanabozho asked her where she kept her medicine rattle in the cave, and when she had told him, he said he would like to hear the song that she sang when she doctored her grandson. So she sang her medicine song, and when Nanabozho had learned it, he killed her and flayed her. Then he put on the Frog Woman's skin, dove into the lake, and swam down to the cave of the spirits.

In the cave, the spirits were in human form, but when they went out they put on animal form, because in that form they had more power. The door of the cave opened only between daylight and dark, when the Frog Woman used to come to doctor Mishi Bizi. Nanabozho was at the door when it opened, and he walked in, dressed in the skin of the Frog Woman.

Two frogs were on guard inside the door. They said: "Our grandmother looks like Nanabozho."

He struck them with the old woman's staff to make them keep still. He said: "It is crying all day that makes my skin so wrinkled."

Nanabozho

He called for the medicine rattle, and singing the song of the Frog Woman, he came close to Mishi Bizi as if to doctor him. Then seizing the arrow, he drove it into the heart of the panther and killed him. Then he ran out of the cave and escaped.

When the flood came, Nanabozho climbed the highest mountain. But the water rose to the top of the mountain. Then Nanabozho climbed a tall pine, but the water rose to the top of the tree. Nanabozho said to the pine: "Brother, stretch." And the tree stretched his own length. Three times, when the water rose to the top, the pine stretched his own length. But the fourth time, the tree said that he could stretch no more. Soon the water reached Nanabozho's waist, then his neck. When it was almost up to his mouth, Nanabozho saw a blue heron and said: "Brother, drink up all the water you can hold." Then the heron took his fill and sank from sight.

At the same time, seeing a beaver, Nanabozho said to him, "Dive and fetch me up some earth, so that I can make a new world." The beaver dove but the water was so deep that he could not reach the bottom. He came up dead, and Nanabozho blew on him and brought him to life. Then an otter swam by and Nanabozho sent him down also to get some earth. But the otter, too, came up dead and Nanabozho blew on him and brought him to life. At last Nanabozho saw a muskrat and said to him: "Brother, dive quickly and bring me up some earth, so that I may make a new world. Otherwise we must all die." The muskrat came up dead, but his paws were closed tight, holding a little earth. Nanabozho blew on him and brought him to life. Then he took the earth brought up by the muskrat and, holding it out on his hand prayed to the Great Spirit for the hottest day that ever came. So the earth dried on his hand and Nanabozho blew it out on the water, and made a new world.

This was the world where we live today. By the flood, the people of the old earth were drowned and the Great Spirit put upon the new earth the father and mother of the people of this earth.

When Nanabozho stepped on the new land, he saw the blue heron lying on the shore with his belly swelled to immense size by the water he had swallowed. Nanabozho kicked him in the belly and the water poured out in such a stream that Nanabozho had to run away to keep from being drowned.

Nanabozho lived many years on the new earth and at last disappeared. Nobody knows where he went, but the Indians do not believe that he is dead, for when they are without food, they can get what they need by praying to Nanabozho. So he must be living somewhere in the spirit world.

Kawbawgam's Remarks on Nanabozho

Before beginning the story, Kawbawgam said: "Nobody knows where Nanabozho came from. If the Indian had been as wise as the Chinese or the French or the Germans, our people would have made books so that we should remember what happened in ancient times. But all that the Indian knows is that there is a creator above, who made the world with everything in it and gave the Indian a heart to know the Great Spirit."

"As for Nanabozho, we only know that he was a man like ourselves. Yet he had more power than any other Indian; he could speak to the water and make it stop and to the wind and make it talk. He called the animals his brothers; men he called his uncles; women and trees and all that grows and all that flies he called his brothers and sisters. So Nanabozho must have been one of the oldest of them all.[6] That is why we can't tell where he came from, any more than we can tell the beginnings of things in the world, because these things were so long ago."

"Once in a while amongst the people there is a very strong man or a good fighter or a wise man; you don't know how he came to be so; you only know that he was the son of a father and a mother. So it was with Nanabozho; he was born of human parents. But no matter where you look amongst any tribe of Indians, there was no one else like Nanabozho. He had some great power; he could do wonders that no other Indian could do. Yet he lived like others; he had a family and camped through the woods, and when there was famine, he went hungry with the rest."

On finishing the tale of Nanabozho, Kawbawgam said: "This Nanabozho had tremendous power. The evil spirits had terrible power too; but they were afraid of him because he was even more powerful. The spirits

---

[6] Because he called the birds, who are spirits, his brothers. Remark by Jacques LePique.

feared him because he could command the rain, water, and fog. As for the story of the flood, I do not understand it.[7] Nevertheless, it shows Nanabozho's power[,] for during the flood the Great Spirit sent a hot day to dry the earth on his hand so that he could make a new world."

"Whether the new world touched the bottom of the flood or not, the old world is below. I do not know whether the water drew off after the flood. That is not in the history."

"Before the flood, there were three gigantic animals in the world, the bear, the skunk, and the mole. They were wicked—destroyed everything they saw. When the skunk went along, it was like a whirlwind. But these gigantic animals came to an end in the flood."

"However, there is a spirit in everything—everything that moves and grows: beasts, plants, clouds, stars, the sun, water, rivers, and rocks. The Great Spirit is the ruler of all spirits. Other spirits have great power but the Great Spirit overmasters all. He made the world and all things."

On another occasion, when I asked Kawbawgam some questions about Nanabozho, he made the following remarks, which complement the foregoing in touching on the droll, tricky, less dignified side of the character.

"Nanabozho was feared on account of his tremendous power but he did not understand how to control his power. He could make a new earth, yet sometimes he acted like a fool, making jokes and playing tricks, though his pranks were harmless. He was able to kill Mishi Bizi, the chief of all the water spirits, yet he was a common Indian. Afterwards he disappeared and became a pure spirit.[8]

---

[7] I think Kawbawgam means that he does not understand, since Nanabozho could command the elements, why he did not stop the flood.

[8] *Editor's note:* Kawbawgam's version of the central episodes of the Nanabozho cycle is closest to that recorded by William H. Ellis in 1888 originally published in the *Varsity* and recently republished by A. Helbig in an anthology entitled *Nanabozhoo, Giver of Life.* Versions recorded by Kohl (1860:432–438) and Schoolcraft (1985:40–45) bear close affinity and likely reflect a sub area of Ojibwa narrative distinctive of the southeastern shore stretching from L'Anse to Sault Ste. Marie.

How Nanabozho Came to Have a Wolf Companion

Jacques LePique

While trying out the fat of a bear that he had killed, Nanabozho was annoyed by the squeaking of the branches of two trees, [that] chafed against each other by the wind. He told them to be quiet and when they squeaked again, he climbed one of the trees to tear down the branches. But as he was forcing them apart, one of his hands slipped and his arm was caught between them and held as in a trap. At that moment, Nanabozho saw a pack of wolves going by and called out: "You can go right along. There is nothing to eat here!" The wolves surmised that Nanabozho had some meat, and coming up, they devoured his bear. Thereafter, fearing that Nanabozho would take revenge on them, they made him a present of a young wolf to be his friend and nephew. (—This narrative was related to my father, Alfred Kidder, in the 1860's.) A similar episode appears in the version of this story recorded by H. R. Schoolcraft (1856:40).[9]

---

[9] *Editor's Note:* In Schoolcraft's version, moose meat rather than that of the bear is stolen and consumed by wolves. The story is equally found in Josselin de Jong (1913:18) and elsewhere but is not generally part of Nanabozho stories linked with the deluge.

Nanabozho in Time of Famine

Kawbawgam

Once in a hard winter, Nanabozho could get nothing to eat. So he went to see his friend the woodpecker, who seemed to have plenty. The woodpecker had built his wigwam around an old pine stub. Knowing very well that Nanabozho was hungry, he took his bird form (till then he had been in the spirit form)[10] flew up on the stub and began to hammer here and there, as we see him do now-a-days. He pecked several holes and pulling out two or three worms, turned them into raccoons, which he dropped into the lodge. Then he came down, killed the raccoons and, throwing them on the fire to singe off the hair, told his wife to cook them. Nanabozho had all he could eat and the woodpecker gave him the rest to take home to his wife and children.

Nanabozho purposely left his mittens. As soon as he was gone, the woodpecker saw them and sent his boys to run after Nanabozho, but told them not to go near enough to hand them to him but to throw them, because Nanabozho was so tricky he might be up to some mischief. What Nanabozho really wanted was a chance to speak to the little woodpeckers; so when he saw that they were going to fling the mittens, he called out: "Hold on, boys! Don't throw my mittens. You'll dirty them on the snow." So the boys came up to hand them to him and Nanabozho asked them if raccoons was all they had to eat.

The little woodpeckers said, "Yes."

"Well, then," said Nanabozho, "tell your father that I invite him to come to see me tomorrow."

Nanabozho was always trying to imitate anything that he saw done. Next day he moved his lodge and built it around a pine stub near by. His wife said to herself that he was going to imitate the woodpecker. And,

---

[10] "That is," said Kawbawgam, "in human form, for that is the natural form of spirits."

sure enough, when the woodpecker arrived, Nanabozho jumped on to the stub and began climbing so fast that he lost his hold and tumbled on his back. His wife thought he was going crazy. Pretty soon he tried again, shinned up the stub as far as he could and butted and banged it with his forehead till he fell down senseless. The woodpecker brought him to, and Nanabozho sat with his head in his hands, thinking. He had no excuse but to blame his wife.

"Since I married this woman," said he, "I have no more luck. I've lost the power I had before."

Seeing all this, the woodpecker took his bird form, flew up on to the stub and, pulling out several worms, which he turned into raccoons, left them for Nanabozho and went home. In a few days, when the raccoon meat was all eaten, Nanabozho thought he would go to see the muskrat, who was living with his wife and children at a small lake in the woods. You know the muskrat has a wife to this day. His hut was built over the water and rose above the ice. He built there because he lives on plants that grow in the water.

The muskrat, in his spirit mind, knew that Nanabozho was hungry and said to his wife: "What shall we give Nanabozho to eat?"

There is a kind of root a good deal like white potatoes that grows in bayous and ponds, and the woman said they would give him some of these. So she went out on the Bayou with her axe and brought in some of these potatoes, but to Nanabozho they looked like nothing but lumps of ice. She put them into a hole in the fire and after a while, trying them with a stick and finding they were cooked, she took out of the coals, not ice but roasted potatoes. The muskrat put them into a wooden bowl and set them before Nanabozho.

"This," says he, "is all we have. Eat all you want."

Nanabozho was watching everything. When he had eaten, he started home, pretending to forget his mittens. The muskrat noticed them and told his boys to take them to Nanabozho but warned them not to hand them to him but to pitch them. "For this Nanabozho," said he, "is so sly you can't tell what he'll do." But when Nanabozho saw that the young muskrat wanted to sling them to him, he shouted: "Wait, boys! You'll dirty my mitts on the snow." So they came up and gave him the mittens, and Nanabozho asked "if all they ate was white potatoes." The boys said: "Yes." "Then," said Nanabozho, "ask your father to come to see me tomorrow."[11]

The next day Nanabozho built a hut like the muskrat's on the ice of a pond. His wife wondered what he was going to do. When the muskrat

---

[11] "And as to that," said Kawbawgam, smiling, "Nanabozho must have had great power to be able to converse with these spirits, for no other man could do so."

came, Nanabozho took his axe and, going out, brought in some chunks of ice. These he put carefully into a hole in the fire, expecting to take out roasted potatoes. Instead of that, the ice melted and the lodge was so filled with steam and smoke that they all ran for the door, tripped over each other, fell down and scrambled out any way they could. That was the end of Nanabozho's feast.[12] The muskrat went home and Nanabozho and his family were as hungry as ever.

With all his power he could get nothing to eat. But at last he thought of a scheme. He invited to his lodge for a dance all that fly through the sky and have feathers. Many birds came. Before the dance was over, Nanabozho said: "We'll dance once more, and when I sing the 'Song of the South,' everyone dance [with] his eyes shut."

Then if any bird dared open his eyes, Nanabozho would wring his neck, and if any bird cried out, Nanabozho shouted: "That's right—sing away! That's how to sing when you dance." But the loon danced on one side of the door and the helldiver danced on the other, beyond his reach. Then they both opened their eyes and cried: "Nanabozho is killing us!"

All the birds rushed out and Nanabozho with them. As the helldiver and the loon went into the river, Nanabozho kicked them from behind and that is how it comes that the loon and helldiver have flat rumps.[13]

Nanabozho had not killed a great many of the birds. Some were so big he was afraid of them. But he had killed enough for several days. He went along the river bank and, making a fire, cooked a meal. When he had eaten all he could hold, he fell asleep with his back to the fire. Suddenly his buttocks spoke saying: "Wake up, Nanabozho. Men are coming." Twice it spoke, but Nanabozho, being heavy with sleep, said: "Keep still. Don't bother me." Then men came and stole his birds. When Nanabozho awoke and found that the meat was gone, he was so angry with his buttocks because it had not aroused him, that he made up his mind to get even with it and, building up the fire, gave it a good burning.[14]

---

[12] The description of this scene Kawbawgam accompanied with a pantomime which set the Indians present in a roar.

[13] Meaning the up-and-down profile of the back and rump of the loon and the helldiver, almost as vertical as that of the penguin, in contrast to the projecting tail of other ducks and geese. The difference is more noticeable when the birds are walking or standing on land.

[14] *Editor's Note:* In the first portion of this narrative, Nanabozho as bungling host together with the forgotten mittens have close equivalents in Schoolcraft (see M. L. Williams 1956:224–227) but are associated with the animal characters moose and woodpecker. Moreover, both themes again appear in Menominee tales of Nanabus and Elk (Skinner and Satterlee 1915:278–282). The duped dancers episode and that of punishing his buttocks are commonly told as separate narratives and, next to the flood story, are the most widely known of Nanabozho tales.

The Diver

Kawbawgam

A very long time ago, before the world (i.e., before the flood) Nana-bozho wanted to get some *migis,* a precious thing (like shells or beads) but he could find no one who was able to get any of it for him. At last the helldiver, Shingebiss, said he would try. Finally, Shingebiss found some migis when he went south for the winter and he used to bring some of it back for Nanabozho every spring. It was thus that the diver came to be called by the nickname, Amiksago, because he brought the migis.[15]

---

[15] This was told to me by Kawbawgam in the summer of 1901 and was interpreted by Paul Pine, the only bit of interpretation of Kawbawgam's words in this collection that was not interpreted by Jacques LePique. The story was elicited by my asking the meaning of "Amiksago" as a nickname for the little boy, Frank Perrot (Mary Cadotte's child) who lived with the Kawbawgams and used to come to my father's with the old man when I was modelling a bust of the latter in 1901. It seemed that as a baby, the boy had a way of bobbing his head up and down like a diver, and the old man gave him the nickname for Shingebiss.

Editor's Note: Within the Midé Society or Midéwiwin, migis shells were presented as a materialization of the Earth's Supernatural, who conceived the ceremony. Migis shells were individually owned equipment used at the climax as a projectile to be "shot" into the patient or placed upon a portion of the body to assure health (Landes 1968:138–140). The helldiver is the pied-billed grebe (*Podilymbus podiceps*) also known as dabchick. H. H. Kidder placed "The Diver" in the appendix as a note to the preceding narrative.

Nanabozho Plays at Being Dead

Kawbawgam

Nanabozho was never sick in his life and did not understand why men died. He thought he would try playing he was dead himself. This was at home among his own family. When a man died, it [was] customary to paint him for his life beyond the grave and to put beside him his knife, his tomahawk, and so forth. These things they wanted to do for Nanabozho, when he made his family think he was dead. But not knowing how to begin, they said, "Where shall we put the paint on him?"

"Why," said Nanabozho, forgetting that he was supposed to be dead, "put it on my eyes."

When he spoke these words, his wife said: "He's not dead yet!" They all began to laugh and Nanabozho laughed, too.[16]

---

[16] Kawbawgam says he does not know what would have happened to Nanabozho "if he had not spoken and had let himself be buried." .

Editor's Note: Nanabozho's playing to be dead and speaking appears in Barnouw (1977:86–88), Jones (1917, 1919, 1:279–299) and Josselin de Jong (1913:21–23) as part of a narrative concerning incest. Nanabozho pretends to be dying and tells his daughter or sister to marry the first man who comes to the wigwam. His burial is faked and in disguise he comes as a suitor but is betrayed by his salutations or a familiar scar and thereafter is mocked by all.

The Lost War Party

Kawbawgam

A war party of seven Ojibwas started against the Sioux in spring as soon as sugar making was over. They walked all summer and all the fall till snow flew. By this time they were hopelessly lost. They could not tell the west from the east—gave up all idea of fighting the Sioux and thought only of finding their way home.

In the night, in camp, they heard singing and a sound like the rapping of medicine sticks. These rapping sticks, which are about a yard long and are covered with pictures, are used by some medicine men in their prayers. They bring luck in hunting and also may give power to find the way in a strange country, but this power only comes after they have been tapped against each other by a medicine man for ten days and ten nights, in the fall of the year, while others sing and dance, praying for the help of Nanabozho.

The chief of this war party set a twig pointing in the direction of the rapping, and in the morning they started in that direction, thinking they might find a medicine man with his sticks. But after traveling all day without seeing anyone, they thought they must have passed on one side of him, and in the evening they camped again. At night they heard singing and rapping of the sticks in the same direction. So the chief set another twig, and in the morning they started once more but again met no one—only heard the sticks as before when they camped at night.

This went on for eight days. On the ninth day, they came to a bark wigwam. The war party, single file, marched in, and saw a man seated on the ground. He seemed to be stupefied. His knees were drawn up, with his feet crossed at the ankle, his chin resting on his folded arms. When he turned his head, his whole body turned with it, as if he were made of stone.

He motioned to the warriors to sit around the fire and taking the magic stick[s], began tapping one against the other, while he sang the song that they had heard at night in the woods.

The warriors thought that the man was Nanabozho himself, in the place where he may remain till the end of the world.

When they had stayed with him four days, he sent them home, guided by a bear. He told them that they must follow the bear for four days, but that on the morning of the fifth day, they must go on alone, taking the direction in which the bear pointed his snout.

The man told them also that just in front of the bear, on the fifth morning, they would see a bush which they should dig up and keep the roots; for those roots, so long as they lasted, would bring success in hunting any game they wished to kill.

On the fifth morning, the warriors went on alone, leaving the bear, and before night they came out of the woods at home.

When told of these things, the people believed, after talking them over with the wisest heads, that Nanabozho had led the war party to his camp by tapping the sticks in order to send them on the right way homeward.

With the roots of the brush that he told them to dig, they were able to get any game that they wanted till the roots were rotted. Thereafter these were of no help. The people searched for some like them but could find none.

The bush was like the life of man, which grows for a time and passes to decay.[17]

---

[17] A very similar version of this story, which I have not recorded, was told to me by Jacques LePique the preceding year on a walk to the falls of the upper Whitefish. Differences that I remember as noteworthy were that the man to whom the warriors were led by the rapping of the sticks dwelt in a huge boulder of sandstone, hollow like a cave, and that on a slab of stone there was roasted game in plenty for the warriors. In Jacques' version, the man himself, whom he called the Stone Man, never ate. That version did not mention the bush and magic root.

Editor's Note: This tale and similar versions recorded by Densmore (1929:99–100), Jones (1919:389) and among the Menominee by Skinner and Satterlee (1915:299–302) depict Nanabozho as an old man dwelling near the world's rim who grants magical gifts to a party of wandering warriors but their requests disappoint them or ultimately disappear.

Thunderbirds and the Medicine Root

Kawbawgam

In old times the Indians believed, and they still believe, that thunder is a bird. This is how they came to believe it.

Once some men journeyed to the Rocky Mountains to find herbs and roots to doctor the sick. They climbed one of the highest peaks, taking long to reach the top. There they found several great nests, each nest holding an enormous bird. But the birds seemed to be babies, for their eyes were still closed. And around their eyes the men saw lightning. One man, taking an arrow, just touched the eye of one of the birds, and the lightning from the closed eye split the arrow.

Before each bird grew a plant. The men thought that these plants must be what they were seeking. So leaving their offerings on one side, they began to dig the roots.

Under each plant, they found a huge frog, lying in a nest formed by the curling roots of the plant. They carefully lifted out the frogs and put them on their offerings, while they dug some of the roots, each man taking a small share, and put the frogs back in their nests. It seems that the frogs were there to guard the young birds. After leaving their presents, the men started away. At the same time clouds began to gather over their heads, and they heard thunder up in the mountains where the birds were.

The men sometimes went there again at that time of year to get some of the medicine root. They would find the birds, make an offering, and dig the roots. A little of this root made a man safe in battle, so that if he prayed to the thunder, he could not be hurt or pierced by an arrow. But once, when they went again, they found that the Thunderbirds, with the frogs and the plants, were gone. The birds had left that place because it began to be too much visited, just as the sparrow hawks, which used

Thunderbirds and the Medicine Root

to nest on Presque Isle,[18] are gone, because there is too much passing up and down the coast.

Even when the Thunderbird was young, he had the power of lightning—enough to split an arrow—but when he is full grown, he has terrible power. The sound of thunder is the bird's voice. He sails overhead, like the gulls, but cannot be seen. When he looks at the earth, lightning flashes from his eyes. He strikes, and then comes the sound of his voice.[19]

---

[18] Presque Isle near Marquette, Michigan.

[19] *Editor's Note:* Thunderbirds, called in Ojibwa *animikig* (Coleman 1961:102), were the eternal enemies of water creatures, and influenced weather conditions, and the hunting of all varieties of fowl. Equally, they were sought as spirit protectors in individual vision quests and because of their swiftness, endurance, and ferocity, associated with war. According to Landes (1968:25), the Arctic Owl and Golden Eagle were assigned thunder traits while Hallowell (1960:19–52) attributes them to the hawk family although they could take on human form. Tales of visits to Thunderbird nests are found in Jones (1917:383–384), Laidlaw (1916:90) and Morriseau (1965:45). Elaborations on this theme include an Indian who became a Thunderbird (Morriseau 1965:6–12), and the Menominee tale of a girl adopted by Thunderbirds (Skinner and Satterlee 1915:350–356).

The Mishi Ginabig and the Thunderbirds

Kawbawgam

The Mishi Ginabig are huge horned serpents that go everywhere under the water and under the land. The finer the weather the nearer they come to the surface; and sometimes when a Mishi Ginabig reaches the surface of the water, a Thunderbird will swoop down to catch him and eat him; or if the Mishi Ginabig nears the surface of the land, a Thunderbird may catch him and haul him out.

There used to be a great many camps along the shore opposite LaPointe.[20] One day about fifty years ago,[21] the people there saw one of these Mishi Ginabig on the surface of the lake. The sky was lowering. Suddenly lightning fell in a stream on the water, and the serpent, after a great struggle, was drawn up by a power that could not be seen and disappeared in the sky.[22]

---

[20] La Pointe du Saint Esprit at the west end of Lake Superior.

[21] This was recorded in 1895.

[22] *Editor's Note:* Generally ranked as an evil manito, horned serpents were associated with drownings, floods, sorcery, and human sacrifice and considered a very bad omen in dreams or individual sightings. Yet they were given a beneficial aspect as a result of sacrifices made to obtain safe passage, good fishing and hunting, and to secure medicinal powers. Horns or tails of these underworld creatures were considered to be made of copper metal. See Barnouw (1977:136–137) and Vecsey (1988:74) for further discussion of attributes or Skinner (1913:81–82) for its equivalent among the Menominee.

Mishi Ginabig in Lake Michigamme

Jacques LePique

A young man named Black Bass[23] asked his father if he had ever heard of Mishi Ginabig being seen in Lake Michigamme.[24]

His father answered: "Well, yes; I've heard that they used to be seen there. I never thought much about it. But they say that if you saw a beaver—cutting on the water in Lake Michigamme, it might show where a lot of beaver could be trapped in the fall."

Black Bass said: "I would like to go to Lake Michigamme to see that for myself."

"If that's so," said his father, "it seems that a man should have a red belt[25] to sacrifice to the Mishi Ginabig. They say that the belt should be put on the water where it will float for a while, and on it should be placed a pipe filled with *Kinnikinnick*. That is an offering to the Mishi Ginabig."

A young fellow, who was listening, said: "I have a red belt. If I lend it to you when you go to Lake Michigamme, why couldn't we trap together this fall? I suppose the manitou ought to be good for the two of us."

So it was agreed. Black Bass started for Lake Michigamme, taking his friend's red belt. He had hardly reached the lake when the water began to boil and he saw the Mishi Ginabig coming up, facing him. The Mishi Ginabig had huge antlers like a moose. His head was two or three

---

[23] *Editor's Note:* Black Bass or Bassfish is given as *ashigân*s by Baraga (1878:I, 23). The same name is associated with a headman of the Carp and Chocolay Rivers in the U.S. Treaty of 1836.

[24] The name of the lake in Ojibwa is Mishi Gawmig, i.e., Big Lake. The local spelling, anglicized and tautologous, is Lake Michigamme.

[25] By red belt is meant the Canadian voyageur's girdle, which went two or three times around the waist and was about a foot wide.

fathoms long and his eyes were tremendous. His body stretched a good part of the way across the pond, although bent in folds, up and down in the water.

Black Bass said: "*Nimisho,* Mishi Ginabig,[26] I wish to make you an offering for power."

He lit the pipe, filled with kinnikinnick, and laid it on the belt floating on the water. The belt then moved from the Mishi Ginabig straight towards Black Bass. It was pointing towards Three Lakes. A stick that Black Bass was holding in his hand showed a great many cuts, the meaning of which was that a great many beaver would be trapped.

In the fall Black Bass and his friend went to Three Lakes and trapped all the beaver they wanted, but they did not take as many beaver as the number of cuts on the stick because their luck was a gift of the spirit.

---

[26] *Editor's Note:* Nimisho is a locative form of *nimishoomis:* my grandfather (J. D. Nichols).

Water Spirits in Sable Lake

Jacques LePique

Once, on the way to Sable Lake, Jacques LePique was wind bound at Grand Marais with thirty or forty Indians and voyageurs.

Yellow Beaver[27] said: "If you are going to Sable Lake, you'd better keep your eyes open. It's a dangerous place—full of spirits. You will see a lot of little tracks on the sand, especially on the northeast side, where the sun strikes. They are footprints of Puk-wudj-in-nin-ni.[28] And you will also see some enormous ones, which are the tracks of great serpents that live in the lake. "Sometimes," said he, "the water goes down, so that there is only a little pond in the center, but the next time you pass, the lake may be full to the high water mark. Don't cross the lake bed when it is dry, for there is no telling when the water might rise. It may come faster than a man could run."

A half-breed named William Holliday[29] said that he had once been there, too, and had seen the tracks on the sand—said that he saw a flock of ducks lighting near the west end and sneaked up to get a shot but that when he had hid behind some logs on the beach, he found "those logs were serpents!"

So when Jacques reached Sable Lake, he was on the lookout and kept his gun cocked. He saw the little tracks on the beach but the water seemed to be about what was probably the usual height. A flock of Teal ducks passed over towards the west end and Jacques crept around to

---

[27] Yellow Beaver, O-za-wa-mi-konce, a brother of Nin-gaw-nub.

[28] *Editor's Note:* Schoolcraft refers to *puk-wudj-ininee* as little wild men of the mountains (M. L. Williams 1956:161, 194); Baraga lists *okadiginebig* as serpents with legs (1878:I, 225).

[29] "This," said Jacques, "was a son of old John Holliday, who had married an Ojibwa girl and ran a trading post at L'Anse."

Jacques LePique, ca. 1880.

shoot—but didn't hide behind any logs! He shot a good many ducks but saw nothing to surprise him.

The Ojibwas believe that this lake has for ages been inhabited by these serpents, which are as powerful as the Mishi Ginabig, though not the same, and that they own the lake and the water. They take the water with them when they leave, so that when they are absent the lake is low, and they bring it back when they return. Now, for a good many years, the lake has been very small, having broken through the sand and run off into Lake Superior. The Indians think that the reason that the serpents have gone away is that they do not like the whites, whom the serpents believe to be as strong as themselves.

The Curing of I-que-wa-gun

Kawbawgam

On the Grand Sable, a young man named Nin-gaw-bi-un was fasting for power from the spirit world. When he had lain for nine days in his little lodge, he heard, one morning, the drumming of a partridge in one of the clumps of woods that are scattered over the sand. He awoke and, crawling towards the sound on his hands and knees because he was weak from fasting, shot the partridge and cooked it in birch sap, for it was early in spring.

When he had eaten the meat, he felt stronger and set out down the coast. At the mouth of the Carp, about twenty miles above the Sault, he met me (Kawbawgam) staying with my father, Black Cloud, [muk-kudday-wuk-kwud] and my step-mother, I-que-wa-gun.

My father told Nin-gaw-bi-un that his wife was very ill; that he feared that she was dying. My father knew that the young man had been fasting, and he made up his mind to give him some tobacco, hoping that Nin-gaw-bi-un could tell him whether there was any chance that his wife would get well. Nin-gaw-bi-un took the pipe and tobacco but said nothing. They turned in at night and in the morning Nin-gaw-bi-un said that he would go to Lake Michigan to bring a great Menominee medicine man named O-na-wa-ban-o. I decided to go with him, and Nin-gaw-bi-un said that we should be gone five days. We arrived the second day late at night.

The next day the old Menominee built a medicine lodge. He had no sooner entered it than it began to shake.[30] Among those looking on

---

[30] *Editor's Note:* Conjuring by means of the shaking tent was performed by Jessakid, a class of medicinemen who acquired special powers during their puberty fast from a principal manito from above or below to cure the sick or find lost objects. Bone tubes and certain medicines which were swallowed and vomited pertained to this ritual practitioner. Various manito attracted by the Jessakid's prayers and songs are said to have come with a wind that violently shook the lodge, then seated themselves on the topmost rung of the

was my half-brother, Muk-kud-de Wi-kan-a-we[31], who had gone to Lake Michigan the year before. He was the son of the sick woman, and he asked the spirit who could now be heard talking, to fly to the Carp and see if his mother was still alive. The spirit was absent about five minutes. He told Muk-kud-de Wi-kan-a-we that his mother was better; she had already taken the broth[32] of a grey duck and that she was going to recover. These spirits seem to be obliged to answer any question.

When the lodge was shaking the hardest, the spirit said: "Is that all you want to ask?" Nin-gaw-bi-un said: "Wait! Here is some tobacco for you to smoke. As we came by Pine River, we set two traps. Go now and see if there are any beavers in the traps."

The spirit was gone a few minutes. When he came back, he said: "There is a beaver in the upper trap belonging to the young man who came with you."

That meant myself.

Said Nin-gaw-bi-un, "You are telling fibs; you had better go back to the spirit world."

Of course he was joking but he knew that the spirit was telling the truth. When they got to Pine River, about half way between Lake Michigan and Lake Superior, they found a beaver in my trap.

The old medicine man went with them to the Carp. There he raised another medicine lodge and of all of the medicine lodges I ever saw none shook so hard as this, and to none came so many spirits, all singing and shouting.

"These spirits are acting so queerly and making so much noise," said O-na-wa-ban-o, "that I think the Great Turtle must have gone under the earth and got some of that whiskey that Black Cloud had buried there in a keg, and must have treated the other spirits for they are drunk."

All were astonished that the medicine man should know about the

---

lodge frame or in a circle on the floor, partook of a drink offering, and then spoke to each other, to the Jessakid and other listeners in their own language or through the medium of the turtle manito. Further reference is made to this form of conjuring in narratives on pages 57, 59, 61, 65, 67, and 149. For complete treatment of the shaking tent ritual see Hallowell (1942). According to John D. Nichols, jessakkiwin (or jisakiiwin in Nicholas' orthography) refers to '"conjuring," operating the shaking tent' while jessakid (or jaasak-iid) means 'the one who conjures," the one who operates the shaking tent.' Both are based on the verb: jisakii (personal communication, Jan. 8, 1991). Kidder uses the two terms interchangeably in the manuscript and they remain unchanged in this edition in order to preserve the integrity of the manuscript.

[31] "Black clothes," meaning a preacher. *Editor's Note: mekatéwikwanaie,* blackrobe or priest (Baraga 1878:I 199).

[32] "When they are sick," says Lahoutan, "they drink only broth."

whiskey that Black Cloud had buried. The spirits in their drunken play tried to pull the Great Turtle out of the lodge but he clung to a pole with one of his legs. When the performance was over, they went with torches and found that some of the whiskey was gone from the keg. Black Cloud asked the medicine man to forgive him for not offering him some of the whiskey before, and presented him with the keg. The spirit said that O-na-wa-ban-o must take care of the squaw for four days. By that time, I-que-wa-gun was cured and they made a feast for four days. When the whiskey was gone the old medicine man returned to Lake Michigan. I-que-wa-gun lived for many years and at last died of old age.

The Great Turtle

Kawbawgam

M i-shi-kan is the spirit messenger, The Great Turtle. This spirit speaks a language that is not understood by human beings. In any operation, he will go to a spirit to interpret for him—in Ojibwa, Menominee, or English. His talk sounds something like the noise of pulling the fingers over a strip of birch bark. He seems to be under the lodge. He brings the spirit of anybody that you want, so that you can talk to the spirit of a friend. If he is not there at first, he will always come. You can hear him tumble into the lodge. You hear his voice as soon as he comes. He must have greater power than the other spirits. The lodge shakes when he comes. He makes a good deal of fun and jokes and plays with the other spirits [who] sometimes try to push him out.[33]

---

[33] *Editor's Note:* Within the shaking tent ritual the nearly unintelligible voice of various spirits is enacted through use of ventriloquism and interpreted by the Great Turtle and the conjuror. The possibilities for general entertainment in this context appear to be limitless. Kawbawgam uses the name Mi-shi-kan, a different turtle according to John D. Nichols, rather than the more widespread usage of Misi-mikinák.

The Girl and the Midéwug[34]

Jacques LePique

An orphan girl of about fifteen was so abused by a couple who had adopted her that she made up her mind to run away and die in the woods. At night, when her foster parents had gone to sleep, she got up and stole from the camp. She walked all night and at sunrise came upon a lake. To the south rose a hill. To the north grew a pine grove, and here she lay down, tired out, and went to sleep.

When she awoke a woman stood before her with a wooden bowl.

"My child," said the woman, "you are not to die here. Get up and eat this meat."

And when the girl had eaten, the woman said: "We have something you must do for us. First, cross the lake in our canoe and take the path up the hill till you come to our lodge. There you will see an old woman who will tell you what to do." Then the woman vanished. The girl went down to the shore, but instead of a canoe, she found a monstrous serpent, a Mishi Ginabig,[35] lying in the water with his head on the beach. She climbed between his antlers, and the Mishi Ginabig swam across the lake, keeping his head above the water, and landed her on the other side.

---

[34] A thorough study of the Midéwiwin among the Ojibwas is presented by W. J. Hoffman (1891). Hoffman gives several traditions on the origin of the society, collected in Minnesota and Wisconsin. The story here related by Jacques LePique, which is quite different from those mentioned by Hoffman, concerns the admission of women to the Midéwiwin, and comes from a section of the tribe living further east on Lake Superior. It was related to Jacques LePique many years before, he said, by an aged Midé of the band at L'Anse, Michigan. This story was read for me at the Folklore Congress in Washington, D.C., on December 8, 1894 by J. Owen Dorsey of the Bureau of Ethnology.

[35] For description of, or allusions to, the Mishi Ginabig see "Nanabozho" [p. 25];"Mishigenabig in Lake Michigamme" [p. 43]; "Water Spirits in Sable Lake" [p. 45]; "The Iron Maker" [p. 69]. Also see "Paying the Devil [p. 65]; "The Man Who Died Three Times" [p. 84].

The Girl and the Midéwug

A trail opened before her and she went up the hill. At the top, she came to a long lodge such as she had never seen before. At the door sat an old woman.

"Come here, my grandchild." So the girl went in and sat down on a mat beside the old woman.

There was no one else in the lodge. Running the length of it, in the middle, she saw a row of seven upright poles,[36] each higher than the next, the highest being at the south end farthest from the door, and on the ground to the right of these she saw seven bags which the old woman called "*Wenimodon,* the lost bags."[37] The old woman told her that the bags and the poles belonged to the seven winds, who were her sons. She said that the pole at the south end belonged to the South Wind; those at the north end, nearest the door to the North Wind; and those between them to the five other winds.

The old woman said: "We have sent for you, my child, because we wish to teach you to be a Midé, so that you may go back to your people and teach others to be Midéwug." This was in the days before there were Midéwug among the Indians.

The old woman said: "We will begin when my sons return. But first I will give you vermilion paint for the ceremony. I am the Old Vermilion Grandmother. Under this mat you will find a tomahawk. You must cut off the top of my head and take out the vermilion paint."

So with the tomahawk the girl cut off the top of the old woman's head and took out the paint that was in it. Then the old woman told her to put back on her head the piece that was cut from it, and said: "My granddaughter, I have given you my vermilion to use in years to come. You must always paint yourself with it whenever you are to perform the ceremonies that we shall teach you. My sons will soon be here. Go now and sit in the place of my son Shawondesi,[38] the South [Wind], for you are to be his wife."

It was now getting towards evening. Suddenly there blew a cold, rough wind from the north, and Kiwedin, the North Wind, burst in at the door. Outside he was a wind but in the lodge he was a young man, very

---

[36] These poles (*Midé Wahtig*) represent, according to Jacques LePique, the seven degrees of the Midéwiwin, which Hoffman, however, puts at four.

[37] "These," said Jacques LePique, "were the sacred medicine sacks used in initiation." *Editor's Note:* The Midé migis sack is called a *wayan* (Densmore, 1929:145–146).

[38] Shawondesi does not mean exactly the South Wind, though the names of the other sons are the usual names of winds. Literally, the South Wind is Shawoninodin. Jacques thinks that the Old Vermilion Grandmother loved the South Wind more than the others and so "gave him a sweeter name." Pet names and nicknames are very common in Ojibwa. *Editor's Note: jáwaninodin,* southwind (Baraga 1878:I,238).

big and noisy. He shouted, "Boju,"[39] and when he saw the girl, he said: "Oh ho! We have a visitor."

After awhile it blew from the east, almost as loud and cold as from the north, and in tramped Wabaninodin, the East Wind. He said: "Boju, boju." Kiwedin [North Wind] said to him: "You see that a woman has come to find us."

Next arrived Ningawbiuninodin, the West Wind, not so cold; and after him came the other winds till all were at home but the South. All at once it grew warm and mild and the old woman said: "Ah, this is my lovely son, Shawondesi [South Wind]. How good he is! When he comes, the air is like spring. He does not come like the rest of you—like bears and wolves."

The young men laughed and Wabaninodin [East Wind] said: "It's true that our brother has a good heart. But another reason is that now he is to have a wife. That's why he comes in like a fawn."

Shawondesi [South Wind] heard this as he reached the door, and he was laughing too. He said: "Boju, boju," and going to his place at the end of the lodge, sat down beside the young girl. He said to them: "We receive her as a Midé, and we will teach her to make Midéwug among the people."

Next morning they began the whole ceremony, teaching her the secrets and all the knowledge of the Midé. They taught her for seven days and at the end, they put a necklace of wampum around her neck as sign of her new powers and told her that whenever she initiated Midéwug among her people, according to the way they had taught her, she should put the wampum before them, as a sacred thing to bind them to their promises.

After seven days she left them to return to her people. She rode back across the lake on the head of the Mishi Ginabig and slept again among the pines. In the morning she was aroused by the sound of voices. Her foster mother, with some other women, was saying: "Well here is that girl, and she has a necklace of wampum around her neck."

"Yes," said the girl, "and where I was given this wampum, I was given power to make Midéwug."

After her return, she built a long lodge shaped in all its parts like the one in which she had been taught, and in it she set up the seven poles. This was the first Grand Medicine Lodge. There she taught the secrets to those that she had chosen, and made them Midéwiwin, and as the first Midé was as woman, there are women in the Midéwiwin to this day.

---

[39] Boju, i.e. *bonjour*. The Ojibwa adapted the French salutation, Good Day.

The Midéwiwin[40]

Kawbawgam

The Midéwiwin is a powerful secret society. Its ceremonies are performed, not in ordinary lodges but in long lodges, like a hall. The members operate either to cure one of them who is sick or to initiate a new member. When there are many members, the lodge is longer; when few, shorter.

They place the person to be cured or the person to be initiated in the middle of the lodge. If a new member has no money or goods, his friends make an offering for him. Presents are hung on a string in the lodge, and as many offerings as are made, so many members come in to take part in the ceremony. A new member is promoted in the society according to the number of members who initiate him. He is initiated as follows: one member first gives a talk and afterwards sings to the Great

---

[40] None of my informants was a Midé or a Jessakkid. The spelling Jessakkid is given by W. J. Hoffman; Baraga spells the word Tchissakid. Hoffman states that, "there are extant among the Ojibwa Indians three classes of mystery men termed respectively, in order of importance, the Midé, the Jessakkid, and the Wabano (1891:156)." Neither Jacques Le-Pique, Kawbawgam, nor the latter's wife mentioned the Wabano. Hoffman writes that "their profession is not thoroughly understood and their number is so extremely limited that little information respecting them can be had."

H. R. Schoolcraft (1855: 1, 319) says that among intelligent Ojibwas known to him the Wabano is considered "of modern origin" and that they regard it as a degraded form of Midé. Hoffman, however, ascertained in the White Earth Reservation, in Minnesota, that the Wabano "does not affiliate with others . . . so as to form a society, but on the contrary, practices individually, in which respect, as in some others, his practice seems to resemble that of the Jessakkid rather than that of the Midé."

Editor's Note: According to A. Skinner, the *wabano* (*wabanowuk,* plural) is a shaman who has the morningstar or the sun as his or her powerful patron, and is known for clairvoyant powers, and demonstrates unusual ability in touching fire and boiling liquids (1913:191–192). Johnston devotes a chapter to the *waubunowin* as a distinct society (1982:113–128).

Spirit, asking for the [Great Spirit's] help and protection of the new member. Then the others speak, till each one has spoken.

The new member is taught all their ceremonies, as if he were at school. He is taught their prayers and songs, which the Great Spirit gives him the power to learn. The Midé have drums as high as a barrel. They make pictures on stones and birch bark, and these pictures can be understood by them alone.

A man who has joined the Midéwiwin at one place belongs to it at any other branch were he happens to be. A person who has been initiated can be recognized anywhere by members of the Midé.

The Midé operations are not performed out of doors. A Grand Medicine Lodge, or at least the frame of one, has to be built. This represents the lodge of the Great Spirit above. The lodge is not a dwelling, it is a temple. And the doings in all earthly Grand Medicine Lodges are heard in the lodge of the Great Spirit in the seventh heaven.[41]

---

[41] *Editor's Note:* For recent studies of the Midéwiwin see publications of Harold Hickerson (1962), Ruth Landes (1968), and an overview by Christopher Vecsey (1971).

The Jessakkiwin
and the Midé

Kawbawgam

Two cousins, living some distance apart, were medicine men: one was a Jessakkiwin, the other a Midé. The Jessakkiwin was suffering from famine, while the Midé had plenty. It seems that the Midé had taken the luck from the Jessakkiwin, for you know that these medicine men sometimes contend against one another, and the one that has more power can get the better of the other by magic.

The Jessakkiwin nearly starved. His wife, being stronger, chopped some wood and set out to find the Midé, for her husband would not tell her where he was. At last she found the trail and reached the camp, [and] saw meat hanging there in abundance. The Midé and his wife asked how her husband was getting along, and she told them that he was starving, perhaps dead.

"Why, why, why!" said the Midé. "So my cousin is starving? Why didn't he use the black coal that he had on his face when he was fasting?"[42]

The Jessakkiwin's wife received from the other woman a present of food, as much as she could carry, and went back to her husband, whom she found still living. When he heard what the Midé had said, he answered: "Oho, he wants me to use the black coal, does he?"

The Jessakkiwin was no longer to be overpowered, because now he was able to withstand the magic of the Midé. He must have had a stronger spirit than the Midé. But like all Jessakkiwin, he would not use his power till asked to use it; he would have died before using it. But when the Midé seemed to dare him to use his black coal, the Jessakkiwin overcame his cousin. And from that time, he and his wife had as much

---

[42] I.e., why didn't he use the power gained in fasting?

game as they needed, while famine began in the other camp. The Midé died of starvation and his wife went to live with the Jessakkiw-in's family.[43]

---

[43] "This shows," said Kawbawgam, "that there is jealousy in all things, even among the Ma-nitous."

The Jessakkiwin

Kawbawgam

A Jessakkiwin is often, though not always, a Midé, and is often more powerful than a Midé. He can foresee events and can cure the sick. The Mushkiwinninnie has nothing to do with magic; he is simply a doctor and cures like a physician.

When a youth fasts to be a Jessakkwin he goes off into the woods to be alone and eats just as little as will keep life in him. Before he goes, his parents tell him not to take any spirit that comes from below, for that is an evil spirit. His parents say: "Take only what comes from above and has feathers."

When the youth is alone, he prays continually to the Great Spirit. If he has faith enough, the Great Spirit will send him power. His power may come in the form of an animal. This animal will say: "I come to help you." If the boy accepts the animal, he takes it as the sign of his power. But if the animal comes from below, he may refuse to take it and wait for another. He may take several spirits as his helpers.

If the youth is unsuccessful, that is, if he hasn't enough faith or enough will-power to stick to his fast, he has to give up and return home. But if he succeeds, he will later become a medicine man and can then use the power that he has gained.

Supposing that there are two hundred boys and girls going out to fast. They must fast while the soul is spotless. They must be over ten years old and must have good habits. In the morning, the sun throws his light over all the earth, but he throws it with more brightness in places where a boy or girl is about to receive power. Not all of the two hundred are to be given power, but perhaps only three of four among them. As the sun rises, he knows which of them are to be given power, for he is sent by the Great Spirit. The fasters to be favored are lying asleep in their little huts in the woods. Here the sun comes to them in human form. It may be a robin, an eagle, a deer, a tree, or even a river or a mountain. The youth, in his trance, sees the spirit before him in the shape of a man, saying: "Whenever you need help, you will see me." Some day, later in his life, when he undertakes to use his power, the animals that he has seen in his fast will again appear and aid him. For instance, if he is hunting for a bear, the spirit of the bear will go through the woods and, seeing a bear in some tree, will come back to the Jessakkiwin and tell him where he can kill the bear. A war party must be led by a Jessakkiwin, for he must be a magician as well as a fighter. By his power, he can not only guide his men, but can also foretell from day to day what is going to happen, for example, how many of the enemy will be killed. If he is going to be beaten, he knows it, but even then he will not stop, for he knows that it is fate, and he will not turn back.

The Jessakkiwin may be sick like other people, but when ill he is helped by his spirit. However, he cannot escape death at last, for when the Great Spirit calls him he must go.

The Cedar Knife

Jacques LePique

Many years ago at Fond du Lac,[44] there was a young Ojibwa who fell in fits. When one of these came on, it took four or five men to hold him. One was a very powerful half-breed named Jean-Baptiste Beaudry,[45] and there were two Frenchmen named Blanchard and DeRocher, besides an Ojibwa called Peter Marksman and Louis Nolin,[46] a half-breed.

When the young fellow came to, after one of his fits, Mary Nolin[47] said to Beaudry, "why don't they get a medicine man for this boy?"

Beaudry turned to him and said: "Suppose we get you a medicine man." And the others all offered to make up a present to give the medicine man, as was often done.

"You needn't do that," answered the young Ojibwa. "I am a medicine man myself, and the time has come to use my power. All you have to do is make two medicine lodges.[48] One standing in water, and one on land." Said he: "I will go into the lodge in the water and come out of the lodge on the land."

The young man belonged to the Lac de Poteau[49] band. It seems that he had a brother who was living in the Rocky Mountains, but he did not know where his brother had gone and did not know that it was this brother who was causing his fits.

---

[44] Fond du Lac, Duluth, Minnesota.

[45] Jean-Baptiste Beaudry was a voyageur widely known on Lake Superior for his great physical strength. He was drowned with Dr. Douglas Houghton, Oct. 13, 1845.

[46] Louis Nolin, the younger son of an Irishman of the same name and an Ojibwa woman, was Jacques le Pique's father. He was an Indian trader.

[47] Mary Nolin, Louis' wife, Jacques' mother. She too was an Ojibwa half-breed.

[48] Conjuring lodges.

[49] Lac de Poteau, Post Lake, Wisconsin; in Ojibwa, Sah-kah-ah-go-ring.

The next morning the men went with him to a meadow on the shore of a pond near Fond du Lac to build the medicine lodges under his direction; and from the remarkable way that he had these lodges built and placed, they felt sure that he must be a medicine man of great power.

The two lodges stood about sixteen feet apart, one eight feet from shore in water about waist deep, the other eight feet from shore on land. The frame of each lodge was made of eight poles driven upright in a circle, and shaped like a straight sided barrel, the same size around at the top and the bottom. The poles, cut from young trees, were sunk several feet into the ground and rose ten feet above it; but in each lodge, one tree on the north side and one on the south side, were left with their green tops uncut. Eight wooden rings were strongly bound around the outside. The frames were then covered outside with red cloth; the tops were covered with white buckskin; and around the top the men tied strings of horse bells. The two lodges were made just alike except that the lodge standing in the lake had a little door above the water, but the lodge on the land had no door or opening of any kind.

Word had got about that there was going to be a big medicine performance, and the people gathered on the meadow a little before dusk. Old Chapman, the Yankee trader, gave a feast, with some whiskey and tobacco, and plenty of clay pipes; and when they had all eaten and smoked, it was getting dark. The young Ojibwa now picked out seven of the strongest men in the camp and called for a brand new rope fourteen fathoms long. This rope had been furnished by Chapman, who had also given the cloth and the horse bells. The young man tied the rope to a handle of a cedar knife about as long as your forearm and three fingers wide. He said that no man on earth could break that knife. "There," said he, "is all my power." The cedar knife, tied to the rope, was slipped into the top of the lodge on land, and the other end of the rope lay nine or ten fathoms along the grass.

"Well," said the young man, laughing, "we seem to be about ready. I will go into the lodge in the water."

He took off his leggings, waded out to the lodge in the water, and got in by the little door. Then he closed the door flap and called to the seven men to take hold of the rope. "Be ready," says he; "and when I give the word, hold hard."

The people had lit torches to see in what shape he would pass from one lodge to the other. Pretty soon they heard him singing, telling how his power had come to him, when he was fasting, and saying that now he wished to use that power. All at once they heard him talking in the other lodge on shore.

He said: "This is just like a white man, to put things in the ground.

I could hardly go through the earth (meaning that the ground had been planted). I almost had to stay underground."

He was laughing to himself. At the same time, the bells on the two lodges tinkled a little, so that you could just hear them. This showed that the spirits were coming through the air, far off.

"Now," said he, "hand in a pipe." The pipe was lit and pushed under the bottom of the cloth, and he told the people to smoke and take some whiskey. While they were drinking, the bells rang a little louder.

"Now we will begin," said he, "for the Spirits are already anxious to come down." As he said this, the two lodges began to shake and sway towards each other, and the bells were jangling so that you could hear them clear across the pond. The seven strong men were sitting on the ground with the rope in their hands and their feet braced in holes.

One of the Frenchmen said: "We'll see what kind of a devil this fellow is."

The spirits were heard talking to the medicine man in the lodge, some like robins, some like crows, some like gray ducks, mallards, and geese. One had a whispering voice. This was the Great Turtle. By and by was heard a tremendous voice. This was the great spirit himself, saying to the medicine man: "What do you wish?"

The young man answered: "I ask you to send the Great Turtle to the spirit of my brother in the Rocky Mountains. He is trying to kill me with fits." This the young man had learned from these spirits. He said: "Let the Great Turtle bring my brother here; and we shall see which is stronger, he or I."

The Ojibwas said: "Let the Great Turtle give us a little dancing before he goes." And they began to strike the drums. With that, the two lodges were seen bobbing up and down in the ground, keeping time to the drums. This was the dancing of the Great Turtle.

Then the loud voice said: "Go," and the lodges stood still, for the Great Turtle was gone.

The medicine man said to the people: "You can smoke. He will not be gone long. He travels fast. He will go a thousand miles while you are lighting your pipes."

After a little while, the lodges began to sway again, and a sound like a hurricane was heard coming, but there was no wind. At the same time, lights like deer's eyes were shining in the west, up in the air. Suddenly the tops of the two lodges came almost together. The turtle had returned, and the voice of the young man's brother was heard saying: "I am here." You could hear him stamp so that the ground shook. He had power, too. He said: "Brother, what do you want with me?"

The young man answered: "You have been trying to kill me. Now we shall find out which of the two of us has the greater power—whether you are going to kill me or I am going to kill you." Then he called to the men: "Hold on to the rope. Hold on strong! I am going to strike him."

The cedar knife on the end of the rope made a noise like lightning splitting a tree. The rope stretched taught and lifted all seven men to their feet. The knife flew out from the top of the lodge and fell to the ground, dripping with blood.

The young man said: "It is done!"

The people made a hole in the side of the lodge on the land, and the young man came out. He said: "We will have another smoke and a drink." "The performance," said he, "is over."

He sat down amongst the Ojibwas like any other man. He said: "If my brother has more power than I, he is alive and will kill me. But I believe that I pierced him through the heart with my knife. When the leaves begin to fall, we should hear of his death in the Rocky Mountains."

The young man fell in fits no more, and, as he said, word came in the fall that his brother had died in the summer.

Paying the Devil

Jacques LePique

A Jessakkiwin[50] in the country northwest of Lake Superior had his
power from Matchi Manido, the evil spirit. In return, he had to give
his children to this spirit. When each child was eighteen months old he
carried it to a neighboring lake, wrapped in a little blanket that he kept,
and threw it from a cliff into the deepest part of the lake.

He had already taken three children from his wife. Now another
was almost a year and a half old and she pleaded with him for its life. She
saw that he wanted to spare it, but he told her that when the time came,
he could not hold back.

He said: "There is only one way to stop me. That is to have someone
kill me. But I warn you that whoever kills me had better look out for
himself when I drop."

The woman told her young brother what the Jessakkiwin had said
and she begged him to help her. The young man was camped nearby on
a river, having lately come up stream in his canoe to fish. He said: "If
your husband takes the child, run and call me."

One morning about daylight, the Jessakkiwin snatched the baby
from his wife, wrapping it in the little blanket, and carried it away towards
the lake. The woman ran for her brother. He seized his bow and cut
through the woods, meaning to get ahead of the Jessakkiwin and lie in
wait for him. The young man was a stranger in that country but the trees
spoke to him as he ran and showed him the way. Soon he struck a path
and the trees told him to stop. So he stood where he was in the brush,
with an arrow on his bow.

---

[50] The Jessakkiwin is one of the three kinds of Ojibwa medicine men, the others being the
Midé and the Mushkiwinninnie.

Editor's Note: Mushkiwinninnie likely refers to medical skills said to be learned

All at once he saw the Jessakkiwin right abreast and let go. The man went down, flinging the baby from him, and as he fell he turned into a snake as big as a tree, in a pool of black stinking slime that boiled out of the ground.[51]

The young man seized the baby and ran with it to his sister. They jumped into his canoe and paddled down river all day without stopping.

After some years, the brother went back to that country on a hunting trip, and on the spot where he had killed the Jessakkiwin he found a bleaching snake's head as long as a man's arm.

---

through visions amplified by purchased instruction, for example, minor healing specialties of herb-brewing, the latter termed by Landes (1968:47) *mashgigiwaboge.*

[51] This was apparently the same reptile as the Mishi Ginabig.

Fasting and Medicine Songs

Jacques LePique

We will suppose that a young man is fasting for power. In his sleep, he hears the air-feathered[52] spirit coming towards him, singing:

"I go with the sound of the wind
Through the world and the sky"

The young man learns that song and repeats it as one of his medicine songs in his Jessakkiwin ceremonies. He sings the song to make the spirit hear him.

Here in our own days, at LaPointe, a young man had been fasting, though no one knew about it, for sometimes it is made a secret. One day, when he happened to be asleep, he suddenly awoke and said to the people around him: "Did you hear that bird? Give me that drum and listen." The bird-spirit sang again and the young man said: "Can you understand?" Someone answered "Why, no." A second time he asked for the drum, and with it, he sang the song [together] with the bird. They could then understand the song as the bird sang it. The song was one that they had often heard the birds singing in the woods, but they did not recognize it as sung by the spirit until the young medicine man sang it with the bird. Spirits come in the form of ordinary birds with the common notes.

When going to battle, the war chief medicine man sings the war song that he heard in his sleep while fasting. Ojibwa songs usually have no regular words; sometimes the singer throws in words here and there as he goes along. The medicine man sings his song to call the

---

[52] I omitted to ask Jacques what he meant by "air- feathered." The words seem to connote something bird-like in the character of the spirits. [See "Nanabozho in Time of Famine," note 10, p. 33.].

attention of the spirits, so that the spirits will come to him and show him the future.

Iron Maker

Jacques LePique

L ate in the fall, a man named Iron Maker capsized with eleven companions off Portage Entry. As he sank he forgot everything, and when
he came to himself he was sitting in a big wigwam on the bottom of the
lake. Near the door sat an old man and an old woman, and a snake as
thick as a man's body lay in a ring all the way around the inside of the
lodge.

The old woman said: "What are we going to do with this man? He
does not belong here."

She had no sooner said these words than Iron Maker was strug-
gling at the surface of the water. He thought of the beaver, whereupon
the beaver came to him and gave him his body. He swam towards the
shore, but before he could reach it, he felt himself losing the power to
keep the shape of the beaver. So he thought of the otter. Then the otter
gave him his body, and in that form he reached land.

There Iron Maker found himself naked in his own body. It was
freezing weather and his camp lay forty miles away on Keweenaw Point.
He would have died of the cold but for the help of four other animals
which, one after another, lent him their bodies to get home: First the
bear, in whose shape he went a good way, then the lynx, then the raccoon, and after that the ox (buffalo).

When Iron Maker no longer had power to keep the shape of the
ox, he was pretty near his lodge. He ran home naked and fell in at the
door half dead with cold.

The animals that saved Iron Maker by lending him their forms
were spirits that had appeared to him when he was fasting in his youth.

Note on Iron Maker

Homer H. Kidder

Jacques LePique said that Iron Maker had long been known as a power-ful medicine man but that late in life he had turned Methodist, at L'Anse, and given up the practice of magic. Thereafter he used to preach to the Indians, and he certainly believed in Christ, but he still believed in the old native spirits, too. He thought, said Jacques, that Christ, being stronger than these, had driven most of them out of the Lake Superior country, and that Christianity had destroyed among the Indians the faith that is necessary for success in medicine operations.[53]

---

[53] In this connection, see anecdote on "The Snow Rabbit and the North Wind," [p. 83].

Kwasind

Jacques LePique

Old Indians say that Kwasind lived about two hundred years ago, on Saginaw Bay. He never married because he wanted to be free to travel about, visiting people, and he fished and hunted only just enough to get what he needed.

Every summer Kwasind made a trip around Lake Superior in a birch-bark canoe. His paddle was of cedar; he would use no other wood for it. He used to start from Saginaw in the spring, cross the Strait of Mackinaw, and coming up St. Mary's River, follow the south shore of Lake Superior around to the west end, and so back by the north shore and the Sault, getting home in the fall.

On one of these trips Kwasind had passed Michipicoten, on the north shore, and was paddling east toward Cape Chaillon. It is a cliff four or five hundred feet high. As he neared the foot of it, he saw a canoe off[shore] on the lake coming towards the cape from the southeast. He wanted to speak to the men in her, but as he ran in close to the rock to meet them, they crossed his bow, holding their heads down so that he could not see their faces. They were spirits who lived in Cape Chaillon. There are spirits in nearly all great rocks and mountains.

Kwasind shouted: "Where are you going?" He did not know that they were spirits. The one in the bow said to the one in the stern: "You look more like a man than I do. You speak to him." These spirits we call *memegwessiwug.* They are about the size of men.[54]

---

[54] Baraga translates memegwessi as "siren (fabulous being)." Dablon in *The Jesuit Relations,* [Thwaites 1889–1901:54, 159] speaks of *memogovissionis* as "marine people somewhat like the fabulous Tritons or Sirens who always live in the water and have long hair down to the waist", a description very little different from *nibawnawbé* of another of our tales [see p. 74]. The beings called memegwessiwug in the story of Kwasind are conceived as rock spirits rather than as water spirits. It is, of course, possible that the words meme-

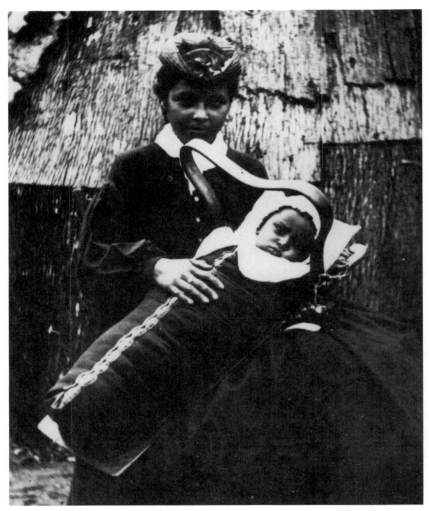

Charlotte Kawbawgam with daughter Monee (Mary), ca. 1860.

gwessi and nibawnawbe were applied to different conceptions in different localities. It is curious, at any rate, that memegwessi are here mentioned in the same region near Michipicoten, where Father Dablon spoke of them in 1669–70.

Kwasind

Kwasind was angry with them because they did not speak to him and he gave their canoe a shove intending to smash it on the rocks. But the canoe disappeared into the cliff as if it were entering a bank of fog. Then he heard voices and the sound of paddles striking on the rock.

One spirit said: "Well, well; so Kwasind thought he could smash our canoe."

Another answered: "Hush! Don't you know that Kwasind is a manitou and can hear us? Keep still." Kwasind went along on his way to the Sault. After passing the rapids, he followed the west side of the river till he came to the head of Lake George. Here on the north side are rocks called *pukwudjininniewug*. When Kwasind passed Squirrel Island, in the middle of the river, the rock opposite rose above him, and he saw little midgets (pukwudjininniewug)[55] running on the ledge. He began joking them, saying they were "no manitous." By the time he was passing along ten miles below, the little men, who had been getting more and more furious over his taunting, picked up stones to throw at him. Kwasind saw one coming and warded it off with his paddle, but the rock broke the paddle. His power must have been in his cedar paddle, for the next rock struck him on the head and killed him.

---

[55] *Editor's Note:* Johnston distinguishes *pukwadjiinineesuk* from *maemaegawaesuk* and *nebaunaube* (1976:167–171). The conflict between Kwasind (Kawaesind) and spirits of sandy lake shores (*paweesuk/pukwadjiinineesuk*) result in death by drowning (168).

Nibawnawbé[56]

Homer H. Kidder

VERSION I

The Ojibwas have a conception apparently similar to those of the mermaid or merman of European mythology. This was brought to my notice last August (1894) in a conversation with Kawbawgam about the genealogy of some of his wife's family. I had asked the name of his wife's grandfather. The old chief at once said, "Nibawnawbé."[57] But when I asked the meaning of the name, Jacques, who was interpreting, seemed at a loss how to translate it. After some talk with Kawbawgam, he said, "It's like a man or woman with the tail of a fish," and indicated by a gesture that these had very long hair.

In my surprise I asked Jacques whether he didn't think the Indians must have got the ideas from fairy stories told to them by white people.

"Maybe," he said incredulously; "but there are Nibawnawbé, anyway. Charlotte saw one in Lake Superior."

Charlotte, Kawbawgam's wife, is a very old woman now blind, the granddaughter of the Nibawnawbé whose name had started the discussion.

It seems that, when a girl, being in camp with her parents at Pickerel Lake, near the place where Marquette is now, she went out to the beach of Lake Superior to get a pail of water when heavy surf was running; and there, beyond the third breaker, she caught sight of a Nibawnawbé. It had the body of a man down to the waist, but the lower part,

---

[56] I noticed that in using the word in speaking English, Jacques said Nibawnawbé for plural as well as singular. The Ojibwa plural is rather awkward or outlandish in English; yet he did sometimes use it, e.g. *Midé wug* and *Puk wudjinineewug*.

[57] Nibawnawbé with its sinister connotation, seems anything but propitious as a personal name. The choice and meanings of Ojibwa personal names, including pet names and nicknames so commonly used, are worth study.

though partly under water, was like a fish. She ran to camp without her pail and would not go back to get it. For to see a Nibawnawbé is a sign that someone of your family is going to die. And, sure enough, her grandmother died within one year.

To this story, Jacques, who had related it, added another. His introduction digressed from Nibawnawbé but seems worth leaving here as a glimpse of Ojibwa boy life two or three generations ago—when Ojibwa boys still told each other stories of fabulous beings.

Jacques LePique said that once as a boy he was peeling potatoes on Sugar Island[58] with another boy named Shawonong [Jawanong].[59] It was hot and between making hills they would lie down in the shade and talk. Shawonong said: "Buk-kaw-kaw-dug,[60] I will tell you a story I once heard." Jacques cut some tobacco from a stick, mixed it with a little Kinnikinnick, and lighting a pipe with fire steel and punk, gave it to Shawonong, because he was going to tell a story.[61] Shawonong smoked slowly, then related the story as he had heard it (in the first person, although the name of Shawonong's informant is not mentioned).

When I was a boy I was once on an island in a small lake in the woods. It was early in the spring and the ice was beginning to melt. I heard ducks quacking in open water on the other side of the island and crawled over hoping to get a shot. But just as I looked out of the woods, I saw two shapes like young women sitting on the edge of a flat rock near the island. They had long hair down to the middle— one had hair that almost covered her shape—and in place of legs and feet they had shapes like fish hanging into the water with tails like scythes. As soon as I saw them, they saw me and dove into the lake. I was so scared that when I got back to the mainland [I] ran all the way home. The old people told me I had seen Nibawnawbé, and one old man said it was a warning of bad luck and that somebody was going to die.

Notwithstanding these stories, I [H. H. Kidder] found myself still doubting whether the Nibawnawbé, which seemed so like the mermaid, could really be aboriginal to America. By chance, I stumbled, next day,

[58] Sugar Island, in the St. Mary's River, below the Sault.

[59] Shawonong (From the South) was Kawbawgam's brother.

[60] Buk-kaw-kaw-duz was one of Jacques' nicknames. It means a thin person, all skin and bones—Jacques, though tough and active, was a wisp of a man.

[61] This seems to have been the custom. When I arranged with Kawbawgam to tell me the stories of his people, Jacques LePique, who was to interpret, suggested the first day that I should take a pipe and tobacco to Presque Isle, to present to Kawbawgam. This I did, and Kawbawgam would always smoke in silence between stories.

on a passage in The Jesuit Relations which seems to afford some evidence on the question. It is in Father Claude Dablon's report to his superior written at the Sault in the Jesuit Relations 1669–70. Speaking of copper found on Lake Superior he relates a fable told him by the Indians, of four savages who in carrying off some pieces of this supposedly sacred metal from a certain island, were rebuked by a terrible voice coming they knew not whence. Some thought it was the voice of the thunder, others that of Mishi Bizi, and still others that it came from Memogovissionis (Memegwessi): these are, they say, marine people somewhat like the fabulous tritons or sirens, who always live in the water and have long hair reaching to the waist. One of our savages, adds Dablon, told us he had seen one in the water.[62]

As a result of the fear inspired by the voice, no one, says Dablon, had been known to set foot on that island "within the memory of man." If, figuring from 1669–70, we allow no more than seventy years for the memory of man, this would take us back to 1599–1600, when there was not a French or English[63] settlement in North America. If then, these "marine people" with long hair reaching to the waist are to be identified with the similar conception described by my informants, we seem to have here presumptive evidence that this conception was an old one with the upper Algonquins when the first Europeans came among them.[64]

VERSION II[65]

The Ojibwa have a conception apparently somewhat similar to that of the mermaid or merman of old world mythology.

I had inquired of Charlotte the name of her grandfather. She answered: Nibawnawbé; but when I asked Jacques what it meant, he

---

[62] This interesting story is one of the earliest, if not actually the earliest Algonquin tale on record.

[63] Raleigh's attempted settlement of Roanoke Island, Virginia, had come to naught.

[64] We still have the unexplained difference between the names applied by Dablon's informants (memogovissionis) and by mine (memegwessi and nibawnawbe). I do not know how widely the conception here discussed was current among the North American Indians. The only mention of such a conception that I have seen occurs in Jas. A. Jones (1830). Also in a journal I kept in Turkestan, a conversation is recited in which a Tajik told us of mermaids of Asian waters.

Editor's Note: Johnston gives a fascinating tale of an Ojibwa who in attempting to rescue a drowning woman was pulled under and lived among Fish-beings who were part human and part fish. According to Johnston, *Nebaunaubaequae* derives from *nebauh* (sleep); *naube* (being), and *quae* (woman) (1976:167–170).

[65] *Editor's Note:* Differences between versions tell us something of Kidder's transcription and editing practices.

seemed puzzled how to translate it. After some talk with the Kawbaw-gams, he said: "Well, it's kind of a man or woman that's half human and half fish"; and Jacques made a gesture that meant long hair.

In my surprise I asked whether he didn't think the Indians might have got the idea from fairy stories told them by the white people.[66]

"May be," he said incredulously; "but there are nibawnawbé anyway. Charlotte saw one in Lake Superior."

"Would you please ask her to tell me about it?" So this is what Charlotte said:

> When I was about twelve, we were once at Pickerel Lake, in the Fall, and one day my mother sent me out to the beach of Lake Superior to get a pail of water. There was a pretty heavy surf. And the first thing I saw was a man in the middle of the breakers, that is, it was a man above the waist but below I could see he had the tail of a fish. I dropped my pail and ran for camp, and when I told the family what I'd seen, they said it was a nibawnawbé. I heard my grandmother say that if you saw a nibawnawbé it's a sign that someone in the family would die. And sure enough, my poor old grandmother died that same Fall.

To this story Jacques, who had interpreted it, added another. His introduction digressed from the Nibawnawbé but it's perhaps worth telling as a glimpse of boy life two or three generations ago when Ojibwa boys still told each other such stories.

Jacques said that once, as a boy, he was hilling potatoes on Sugar Island with a boy named Shawonong. It was hot, and they would lie down in the shade and talk. Shawonong said: "Buk-kaw-kaw-dug, I'll tell you a story that I once heard." Jacques cut some tobacco from a plug, mixed it with a little Kinnikinnick and lighting a pipe with fire steel and punk, handed it to Shawanong, because he was going to tell a story. Shawonong smoked slowly, then told the story as he had heard it, that is, in the first person. He did not name his informant.

> When I was a boy, I was once on an island in a small lake in the woods. It was early spring and the ice was beginning to melt. I heard ducks quacking, in open water on the other side of the island and crawled over to shoot. But just as I looked out of the woods, I saw two young women, as I thought, sitting on the edge of a flat rock quite near the island. They had very long hair—one had hair that almost covered her—but in place of legs and feet, each of them had a fish's tail, which I could see like scythes in the water. I'd hardly got

---

[66] Jacques had told me, more than once, that he loved "fairy stories" by which I think he meant Old-World Fairy Stories.

a look at them when they saw me and down they dove into deep water. I wasn't stopping to shoot any ducks! When I got back to the mainland, I ran all the way home. The old people told me I'd seen nibawnawbés. One old man said that it was a warning of bad luck and that someone was going to die.

The next day, reading in the Marquette public library, I ran by chance on a passage that answered any doubt that one could have regarding the authenticity and originality of the Ojibwa tradition, namely, that of the mermaid or merman. The passage in question occurs in Claude Dablon's report to the Jesuit Superior General at Quebec in 1669–70.

Writing of copper, which he believed would be found on Lake Superior, Father Dablon relates a fable told him by the savages of mythical beings which were "fabulous tritons or sirens, who always live in the water and have long hair reaching to the waist."

Fear inspired by dangerous spirits had kept the Indians from setting foot on a certain island in Lake Superior "within the memory of man." Dablon's report was made in 1669–1670. Man's memory would go back, one may safely say, for seventy years, i.e., to at least the year 1600, at which date there was no French or English settlement in America. In other words the story told by Charlotte Kawbawgam and by Shawonong's informant were evidently of native, not of old world, origin.

A Famine and How a
Medicine Man Saved the People

Kawbawgam

Sixty-five or seventy years ago,[67] a band of Ojibwas were camped in winter on Sugar Island[68] in Lake George below the Sault. In January there was famine. All the people were fishing and hunting but no one could get anything. They had not had a bite to eat for three or four days. When the famine grew so bad, someone said that Nin-gaw-bi-un, a middle aged man in the camp—was a medicine man.[69] That evening several men went to his lodge and found him as hungry as the others. When all had smoked, they offered him tobacco and a pipe.

One of them said: "Nin-gaw-bi-un, we hear that when you were fasting, you received medicine power." Nin-gaw-bi-un laughed. He said: "I accept the tobacco."

They wanted him to show them where they could get some game or fish, but he told them to come back the next evening.

Early the next morning, the people saw someone moving about on the ice off the island, and by and by they saw Nin-gaw-bi-un coming ashore with a big sturgeon on his sled. He went to his lodge and, cutting up the fish, put the whole thing into his kettle—head, guts, fins, blood, and all.

In the evening a messenger invited the people to come to his lodge. They sat around the fire and ate the fish on pieces of wood, though it was not much to feed so many ravenous people. On the ground beside Nin-gaw-bi-un lay something about twice as big as your thumbnail. It was the dried skin of a little bird. He asked the people what they thought so

---

[67] Roughly about 1825 to 1830. This was recorded in 1894.

[68] On the south side of the ship channel in Lake George.

[69] Nin-gaw-bi-un means the West. The same name was borne by another medicine [?] man who appears in another of these stories [p. 48].

small a thing could do. "When I was fasting in my youth," said he, "this bird came to me and said, 'If ever you need help, I will aid you. But if I am not able to help you I will call the Thunderbirds. There will be thunder and rain, and what you need will come.'"

Everyone had a little of the fish and then went home. Next morning, Nin-gaw-bi-un led the men onto the ice and said that, through the bird, he could get food for all. Soon he stopped and told them to cut holes in the ice; and in that one place they speared enough sturgeon for the whole camp. I was there as a boy. One of the sturgeon was as black as charcoal, another snow white; but otherwise these two strange sturgeon were just like the rest.

The people now had plenty, but Nin-gaw-bi-un invited them to his lodge again and gave them a mess of sturgeon, also made of the whole fish. He put the skin of the bird beside him and some tobacco in front of him. Then, before the people began to eat, he sang the song of the bird that had come to him when he was a boy, fasting on the mountain.

He said: "Although it is winter, we shall have tomorrow one of the greatest thunder storms ever seen in this country."

It happened as he said. There was tremendous thunder, the snow was half melted, and the ice was overflowed. After that there was no want of game and fish all winter.

I don't believe that it was the little bird that did all these wonders, but a spirit that came in that form.

The Ojibwas in that camp must have had great faith, for now-a-days if you took a hundred skins on the ice, you could not get a mouthful.

Fragment of a Medicine Story

Jacques LePique

That was when we lived at the Sault. Our house stood about half way along the canal and Kawbawgam's people lived on the point opposite a little island in the rapids.

That morning Kawbawgam and I were out in a canoe in the rapids, fishing for whitefish with a scoop net; and when we started ashore at noon, we saw that some Chippewas had camped near by. One of them was a young fellow about fifteen who had a red plume of hair fastened on his head. He went towards the point with a pole on his shoulder, and when we came along, he was fishing from the rocks. Another man in the party was an old Indian called by the French Shalot Toulouse. He was just going in to see Ka-ga-qua-dung (Kawbawgam's stepfather) and after talking a while he looked round and saw Kawbawgam's mother lying in the corner.

He said: "Who is that? Who's that lying over there?"

The chief said: "That's my wife."

"And what's the matter with her?"

The chief said: "I'm afraid it's consumption. I don't know whether there's a remedy for that disease."

"Well, I don't know," said Shalot. "I wish you'd go and give a pipe to that boy fishing on the point. That boy's a devil of a fellow." "Maybe," says he, "that boy can help her. Maybe he can do something for your wife."

Well, Ka-ga-qua-dung took a pipe—the pipe of peace, we call it— filled it with Kinnikinnick and gave it to us to take it to the boy. So we went down on the rocks and offered it to him.

He looked at us and said: "I don't know if I can accept that pipe, my friends, my time is not yet up," says he. "It's the Great Spirit himself that came to me in my dreams when I was fasting. Well, I'll take the pipe but I have no medicine rattle."

I said, "We can make one in a few minutes." I was used to making them.

So I went home and asked my father for a tin powder flask. He wanted to know what I was going to do with it and I told him that a medicine man was going to doctor the chief's wife. My father said he would come to see the performance.

I went back and said to the boy. "What shall I put into the [cavity], shot or what?" "Oh no, nothing," said the boy. "You put a cork in the flask and raise it on a pole, and the Great Spirit above will put rattlers in it. Light a pipe when you get it up on a pole. If the rattlers come into the flask while I am smoking the pipe, we can cure the chief's woman. But I don't know, because my time was not to begin till I'm married and have one child." "But," says he, "we'll try anyway."

The boy began to smoke and we no sooner raised the flask on the pole than we heard rattlers jingling in it. That was a miracle.

"I will come this evening," said the boy. "You must get a white cloth for the place where the spirit lives is very clean. And I want two candles and a piece of blue ribbon about that long" (Jacques held his hands about a foot apart) "because the place where he lives is sky-blue, I want seven crackers and a little wine (about a pint) in a dish and also whiskey (less than a pint) in another dish."

He said that when he came in the evening he would put into the whiskey-dish seven bones which he would bring himself.

In the evening he came to operate. He began to tell about his (fasting?).[70]

---

[70] The rest of this story is missing, through the loss of one or two sheets at the end of the note-book in which I took it down. My recollection is that in the operation, the boy put in his mouth the little hollow bones which he had previously placed in the whiskey dish, and by applying them to the woman's body, sucked out the disease and cured her.

The Snow Rabbit
and the North Wind

Homer H. Kidder

My father [Alfred Kidder] told me, some years ago, an anecdote that showed the tenacity of Ojibwa concepts among the more or less Christianized half-breeds of Lake Superior. In his exploring trips in the [eighteen] sixties, he often had Jacques LePique as cook. One morning late in the winter, when they were breaking camp for a long tramp along the coast, a thaw promised to make for heavy snow shoeing. Before they left, Jacques took some moist snow and fashioned a rabbit standing on its haunches on the shore facing the north.

The rabbit had an absurd, rakish air, and my father asked Jacques what it meant. Jacques said that the rabbit was intended to make the north wind blow, for Ka-bi-bo-na-kay (the north wind)[71] would think the rabbit was making fun of him and would try to blow him down, but, of course, the colder it blew the harder the rabbit would freeze.

Captain Joe Bridges, who was of the party, asked Jacques if he really believed that nonsense. Jacques said: "Just wait and see." As a matter of fact, when they had gone several miles, it came on to blow from the north and began to freeze. Jacques was elated. He said to Bridges: "Didn't I tell you? It never fails."

Jacques afterwards told my father that this was an old practice with the Ojibwas to stop a thaw at sugar making time.

---

[71] *Editor's Note: kiwédin*, northwind (Baraga 1878:I, 181).

The Man Who Died Three Times

Jacques LePique

A man called several of his friends to his camp and said to them, and to his wife: "I am about to die and I must tell you what to do when I am dead. Three times I must die and each time remain dead for three days. Here is a new blanket, never used. Sew me up in it like a bag and throw me into the river. But tie a line to the blanket so that we can pull it in after I come back. On the third day, you must all be here."

When the man died, they did as he had asked them. On the third day, they were all at his camp in the evening. About dusk they heard someone coming. He entered and looked around, he had some tobacco in his hand and did not seem to be wet.

He sat down and, after smoking his pipe said: "I must die twice more. I should come back each time. When I die," he said to his wife, "do not bury me for if you put me in the ground, I cannot return." They went to the river and pulled in the blanket. After a while the man died again and they sewed him in the blanket once more and threw him into the river.

He had said to his friends: "Do not go to look at the blanket in the river. Wait till I come back."

But next day, a stubborn-headed man went to the river to look at him. What he saw was a monstrous snake with antlers and enormous eyes. Then he knew it was the power of the evil spirit that had brought the man back. He ran away in fright and told the people.

The next evening, the man returned. When he died the third time, they were afraid to put him in the river because of the Mishi Ginabig. So they buried him in the ground.

The Man from the World Above[72]

Jacques LePique

A ges ago, a young man said that he came from another world above. In that world (you will go there after you die) you cannot wish for anything twice without getting it.

"When I was there, I saw you down here, dancing and playing, for we could see you down here and could hear you talking at which," he said,

> I am astonished. I did not know then that I could have whatever I wished. But in my heart, I wished that I could be down there amongst those people, they seemed to be having such a good time. That passed, but when I felt that wish again, I saw before me a spirit form in white. This spirit must be one of the sources of *Kitchi Manito*. He said, "You have wished twice to go. Now you may go. But here is the commandment for you when you are there: You must not steal; or lie or talk evil of anyone but have only good thoughts and do good." "And there," said the spirit, "you must pick out the fairest and cleanest couple you can find to be your father and mother." All at once, as quick as an eye can flash, I was here. I walked around. Nobody looked at me. When I spoke, no one answered. Then I went close to someone and spoke in his ear. The person only said, "Oh, how my ear rings!"

"Whenever," said he, "your ear rings, it is because a spirit from the other world is speaking to you."

"At last," he said, "I thought of the commandments that had been given me [from] above. I looked all about among the people. I could see

---

[72] Although details in this section of our manuscript contain Ojibwa ideas, it is evident that the following is not native Ojibwa lore. The resemblance to the Christ story seems obvious.

the heart of each and know which ones were the best. I chose the most virtuous man and woman on earth and I was born again from them. I knew nothing for a time, when I was to be born again. But when I was born, I heard an old woman say to my mother: 'Here is a man that comes from the spirit world.' One man asked how she knew this. She said: 'It is easy to know. When you see a child that is born with a mark on his body, such as a vine or tree or any other special mark, you may know that he had that mark in the other world, and has been born again.'"

The young man grew up like others. But he played mostly with the children and was very quiet for fear he might fall into some temptation to break the commandments given him [from] above. That is why he was so much with the children, even after he grew up. Everybody noticed this and wondered at it.

One year a great famine came amongst the people. They had nothing to eat for many days. Some were already dying. Then someone took tobacco and went to medicine men for help, to get game or fish. But no one felt enough power to take the present. At last one medicine man accepted the tobacco, and after smoking said: "Do you see that young man playing among the children? He can help you." This medicine man had seen the young fellow's power by his own spiritual sight. He said, "Go and offer him tobacco."

Someone did so and asked the young man if he would not have enough pity for the children and the other people to look for something to eat for them.

The young man answered that he had no more power than any other man. "The only one that has power is the Great Spirit above us all. I have no more power than you. But I will ask one question. Do you know why you are hungry now?"

The man said: "No."

"It is because when you have things in plenty you waste them." He pointed to a number of young men and said: "These men have had fish and game in abundance and have wasted it. The Great Spirit has seen this and wishes to punish them and that is the reason of the famine." "But now," said he, "we must speak to the Great Spirit and ask his forgiveness. Tomorrow we shall all remain quiet and each man must think of nothing but the Great Spirit, praying to him to give us food. And tomorrow you can come to me."

The next morning when they came, he pointed to a long point in the lake.

"It is very calm," said he, "you can paddle over there. But take your sails so that you can sail back for a fair breeze will spring up at noon to carry you home." When the party returned, they brought a great store

86

of sturgeon, trout and other kinds of fish. There was then gladness among the people. After their feast, the young man said: "Always take care of what the Great Spirit gives you. Never waste again. These fish and everything that you see moving on earth are all meant for you to use. There is a spirit who does nothing but watch the game, and if you waste it, the Great Spirit will be angry and will punish you."

"In the world above," said he, "the flowers smell sweeter, the rivers are grander, the sun, moon and stars are brighter. There is a blue sky as there is here. But that is not all. For there are six skies above that, each one finer than the one above. The highest, above them all, no man can know for that is the home of the Great Spirit himself." This was the end of his preaching. He played among the children as before. Time went on till, some years later, there was another famine. It was in summer, like the other. The people went to him again. He said, as before: "I have no power. You must speak to the Great Spirit. The pigeons are eating all the huckleberries. We must not speak a word today but remain silent thinking of the Great Spirit, asking him to send us aid."

The next morning he spoke to the pigeons, where there was a great flock of them near a tree. He said to them: "See how our children are suffering. They are nearly starved. You have wings. We have not. Therefore, you should go to some other part of the world, where there is food. Do not eat up all that there is here."

The pigeons all flew away and from that day, no pigeons were ever seen in that place. The young man had always foretold his death. Every time he now preached, teaching the people to be good, he said that he had not long to live.

A day when the sun was hanging half way in the heavens, he knew from the spirits that the time was come when he should tell his father and mother that he must leave them. Of this he had warned them before but their grief was hard to bear, his own not less, for he loved them. He asked his mother to tell his friends, one friend especially. But all were very sad. They said: "Is it true that our friend, the good spirit, is to leave us?"

He said: "Yes, I have to go. I came here only for a while. I do not belong to this land. But when I die, you must all go to the top of that hill," to which he pointed.

So the people gathered at the top of the hill. They sat in a circle, smoking. The young man lay in the center near his friend. He said to him: "What shall I do for you? I wish to leave you something."

His friend said: "The best thing that you can leave me is the power that you have had." The young man asked his mother if she had brought his bag. She said: "Yes," and gave it to him. He took out a buckskin jacket and gave it to his friend saying: "As long as this coat lasts, you will live and be able to use my power." He said to his father and mother: "This is to be your son after I die." And he said to his friend: "These are to be your mother and father."

Then as the sun reached the center of the sky, he suffered pain and passed away. He had said to his friends that he would come to the Earth again, but did not know when or where. "When I come again," said he, "the end of the world will be near."

The Robin[73]

Jacques LePique

In autumn, a boy was fasting for power from the spirit world. Through the spirit that came to him, he knew that he had fasted long enough and told his mother that it was time to stop. But she urged him to keep on and would not let him out of the lodge.

The next day he said: "Mother, I have fasted too long. I can no longer be a man. I shall become a bird and must leave you."

His face and throat were painted black, with a few white specks, his breast was painted red, and on his back he had a covering of grey. All these marks he kept when he became a bird. He flew out, and perching on the lodge, gave the beautiful call of the robin.

He said: "Whenever you hear me at the top of a tree, you will know spring is coming and will come always to the end of the world. Farewell, mother. I am going to spread throughout the earth."

This was the first robin. His descendants are seen everywhere.[74]

---

[73] This is, of course, the American robin.

[74] Recorded by my brother, Howard White Kidder. *Editor's Note:* The origin of the robin (*pitchi*), associated with the over-bearing influence of a parent or grandparent interferring with a vision quest, is likewise recorded by H. R. Schoolcraft (M. L. Williams 1957:106–107), by H. Gerald Turner in A. K. Helbig (1987: 210), and in its most elaborated form by Basil Johnston (1976:128–131). According to Morriseau, the robin's call is understood to say in Ojibwa language *neeshewukjeebeyuk,* "two dead persons," thereby linked to a narrative where it finds the bodies of two youths lost in the forest (1965:84). In the Kidder manuscript, the song of a robin is given as wash-ka-ka-ka-ka (p. 149).

The Whippoorwill

Charlotte Kawbawgam

The Whippoorwill was once a child. His mother went one day to visit friends, leaving him with strangers. He was afraid and cried all afternoon. You know babies will sometimes cry and cry till they catch their breath and hiccough. So it was with this one. But in the evening he suddenly stopped crying.

"Hereafter," said he, "you shall hear my song at twilight."

With that they saw a bird fly out. He was the first whippoorwill. The child had a collar of white buckskin. You can see it on the whippoorwill to this day. And if you see a whippoorwill and look closely, you can see the tears coming from his eyes. He is weeping still.[75]

---

[75] *Editor's Note:* The singing of the whippoorwill close to the lodge foretells a death in the family. It is a messenger from the evil powers as is the sighting of a mermaid (Skinner 1913: 83).

The Sister's Ghost

Charlotte Kawbawgam

A young man lost his wife. Her body was put into a square covering of split cedar bound with bark, and was placed on a high scaffold, as they used to do sometimes in those days. This was perhaps hundreds of years ago.

Not long after his wife's death, the man married her young sister; and by and by the old man, his father-in-law, saw that the dead woman's covering was open. He said nothing about it but wondered how this had happened.

Just at that time a strange woman came to the encampment—the dead woman it was—and one day asked the second wife to go into the woods with her to gather kink root for soup. At first the young wife did not want to go with her but as the stranger urged her, [she] said she would go. They walked for a while and made a fire to cook something. But when they sat down to eat, the young wife was terrified to see the strange woman eating the coals and flames. She fled in affright, calling to her mother to save her.

She cried, "I am chased by a spirit." "Yes", shrieked the spirit. "I am the ghost of your sister. You married my husband and I will kill you."

When the family heard the cries, they opened the wigwam door. But the ghost was close behind and pushed the live woman into the fire in the middle of the lodge, where she was burned to death. The spirit then vanished.

From that day to this, amongst the Indians, no man whose wife dies would dare to marry his sister-in-law.

The Beast Men

Jacques LePique

In old times, when game was so scarce that people had to make a long move, if an old man or old woman or some old couple gave out on the way and could not go on, they had to be left to die, with any food that could be given them.

But one old man who was thus deserted made up his mind that he was not going to sit there and starve. When he had eaten what food was left, he got up and started away. He had nothing to carry but his staff. He went along slowly but kept on for three days, and the third day he came out of the woods on the Grand Sable above Lake Superior.

From the look of the place, he saw that it had been a big camp-ground, but there was then only one wigwam. He went to the door and looked in. A voice said, "Come in, Grandfather, and sit down." This voice came from behind a partition in the lodge. It said: "Rest yourself and eat. There's meat hanging by the fire. I can't come out, but my brothers will soon be home."

So the old man sat down and ate. After a while six young men came in from different directions. The oldest brother, Machikiwis, who came in from the north said: "Boju[76] Grandfather. Has our youngest brother asked you to eat? He is behind that partition, fasting for power to help us."

"You see, Grandfather, that there are not many of us. Once, hundreds of wigwams stood on the Grand Sable and all along the lake shore. But every so often we have to run a race, and now there are only seven of us left."

This puzzled the old man. He said: "I don't understand what you mean about racing."

---

[76] Boju i.e. bonjour.

The Beast Men

The oldest brother, Machikiwis, said: "Well, I will tell you about it. There are beings around us here in the woods who are able to take the form of either beasts or men. Every so often they dare us to choose one of us to race with one of them and to bet so many lives on the race. We have lost every time. Here are all of us that are left."

The old man asked what the other party did with the people they won in these races. Machikiwis told him that they killed them and ate them.

"Behind that partition," said he, "our youngest brother is fasting for power hoping to win the next race."

By this time the oldest brother, the one who had come in from the north, had filled a pipe and putting fire to it, held it out to the old man. The others watched to see what the old man would do; for if he took the pipe, it meant that he had medicine power and was willing to help them.

He said: "I accept your pipe."

Taking it, he smoked, and said: "What if I race for you?"

The brother shouted: "Megwuk! We all thank you![77]

Machikiwis cried: "Our Grandfather is going to race for us." And he said to the old man: "How many of us will you bet?"

Before this each side had bet the same number of lives. But the old man said: "We will bet half,"—meaning that the other party numbering thousands, would also have to bet half. "If we win," said he, "there'll be plenty of meat. The deer and partridges and rabbits amongst those fellows would make a pretty good bouillon." He was laughing but when he [was] done joking, he asked Machikiwis if they had some red paint, and said: "I want you to make me a wooden ring, very strong. If we win, it will be by that wooden ring."

Machikiwis went to work and made the ring. And when the moon was so many days old, he said: "Grandfather, the race will be tomorrow."

He led him out to the bluff of the Grand Sable, over the lake, and showed him a point called Lonesome Point[78] about fifteen [five] miles beyond Grand Marais, as you go towards the Sault.

Machikiwis said: "The race is run from Lonesome Point to the Grand Sable. You walk down there and race back to this pole." He showed the old man a pole set up in the sand with a bunch of feathers hanging at the top.

---

[77] *Editor's Note: migwetch* (Baraga 1878: II, 235).

[78] Lonesome Point was called by the Ojibwas Ne-te-sage-wa-a-zingh, which Jacques translated "The point you never get around," i.e., in passing it, for six or seven miles, you still see the point curving beyond—an experience anyone will remember who has done much rowing along the coast of Lake Superior. The name would fit many other points.

Early the next morning, the old man painted the ring red. With six of the brothers he went out to the edge of the Grand Sable. The youngest brother, though counted in the bet, did not go because he was fasting. When they reached the bluff, the animal party, all in human form, were waiting for them in thousands; they stood in rows so long that you could not see the end of them. They had their "Oldest Brother," too. He is the one who generally does the talking for his side. He said: "Oho, here's our Grandfather. Is he going to race?" For they saw that the old man was painted and decorated. "Yes," said Machikiwis of the brothers. And the men of the beast party shouted: "Oho, Grandpa's going to run!" And all laughed and clapped their hands.

"Well," said the oldest brother of the animals, "here's our man." And he shoved out a young sparrow hawk in human form. The sparrow hawk, Ka-Ka-Ki[79] shook hands with the old man and said: "Let's go. It's a long way to the starting place."

The old man went along with his stick, carrying his red ring, and at last they reached Lonesome Point. Here was a deep pit, and the racers had to start from the bottom of it. When they got down into it, they took a rest and a smoke.

"Well," said Ka-Ka-Ki, "are you ready?"

"Yes," said the old man. "Go!"

He had no sooner spoken than he saw a sparrow hawk fly out of the pit and head for the Grand Sable. He climbed out of the pit and threw his ring into the air, saying to it: "Fall half way to the Grand Sable." With that he flew into the air, and afterwards told his friends the brothers that he had passed over the blue back of the sparrow hawk. When the ring came down on the shore, the old man landed beside it, and throwing it into the air again, said, "Fall by the pole where the feathers hang." There he landed before the sparrow hawk had passed Grand Marais. The older brother of the animals said: "You have won. You can begin to kill."

The brothers took knives and tomahawks, meaning to kill half of their enemies. But the old man said: "Wait, my sons. Let us race with them again, and we will bet all our lives against all of theirs."

So they had another race the next moon. This time the old man and his ring were painted blue. He raced against the winter hawk, and won again, flying through the air after his ring. The brothers had now won the lives of all their enemies, but the old man would not let them kill. He made all the animal party pass before him, one by one. He forbad them

---

[79] *Editor's Note: Kakake* (Schoolcraft in M. L. Williams 1956: 253); *kekeke* (Baraga 1878:II, 239).

ever again to take the form of man, and told each kind how they should live and what they should eat. And that is how the animals got the habits that they have to this day.

The Great Skunk

Kawbawgam

The skunk was once as big as a mountain; he could be seen a hundred miles away. Wherever he passed he left a clean sweep, the trees all broken down and every living thing was poisoned. At last the fisher called a council inviting the mink, the wolverine, the martin, the badger, the squirrel, the chipmunk, and the weasel.

The fisher was chief. He said: "If we do not kill this skunk he will destroy everything in the world. Let us make an ambush and attack him all together."

Having agreed on a plan, they waited where the skunk was going to pass; and as he came along they rushed out at him. The fisher, the wolverine, the martin, and the badger leaped at his throat, the weasel and the mink got into his bowels, and the chipmunk and the squirrel jumped down his throat and gnawed his heart.

Thus they killed the great skunk, and began to tear him in pieces. But the pieces turned into small skunks and ran away. These were the fathers and mothers of all skunks in the world.

In the fight, the skunk had thrown his stench on the animals attacking him, and you can smell it a little even now when you skin any of these, especially the weasel. Each of them still wears sign of victory: the weasel has a brown coat in the fall, which in winter turns pure white; the squirrel has a fine red coat and a bushy tail; the chipmunk has pretty stripes on his back; and the badger has bright streaks of yellow and black around his mouth.

The Great Bear
of the West

Kawbawgam

A man on the north shore of Lake Superior had the gift of great speed. He could travel faster than an arrow shot from a bow. Yet he did not understand his own power.

This man had a dream four nights running; each night the dream went on where it had left off in the morning. After the second night he said to his wife: "I am dreaming of a monstrous man from the north." And the fourth night, towards morning, he thought he heard the man's footsteps coming. He felt that the man had power to kill him and that he could not escape; but whether the man wanted to hurt him, he did not know.

He awoke and told his wife that a giant was coming from the north. They ran out in fright, for it is known that giants will eat people; and in the dawn they saw him a long way off coming with fearful speed, taller than the tallest pines, but the nearer he came the smaller he seemed, till at last, when he was near enough to speak, he seemed no taller than an ordinary man. This frightened them more than ever.

The giant said, "Don't be afraid, my friends, for I have come to see you. I am the man of the north. I am going on a journey to the great bear of the West, to take from him the belt of wampum which he wears, for it is the richest wampum in the whole world."

The giant laid down his war club and a sack that he carried on his shoulder and said to the man, while the women and children sat listening, "You are the only man on earth who can travel fast enough to make this journey with me, and I want your aid. Many have lost their lives trying to rob the wampum from the bear, but I think that, with your help I can take it from him."

The giant said to the woman: "Do not fear. We shall return before evening." Yet in his own mind he was not sure that they should return. He said to himself, "If we do, we shall be the first."

All at once the giant took his full height and picked up his club and his bag. Off they started. But as fast as the man went, he could not keep up with the giant.

"Faster!" said the giant. "Come on, faster!" He had in his sack the feathers of the swiftest birds—though his own speed was not from the feathers—and he gave some of them to the man. When the man had taken them, he went faster but he was still behind. Then the giant gave him the feathers of the sparrow hawk, but that was not enough. The man said: "Give me the feathers of the winter hawk." But even with these, he was not going quite fast enough. So the man said: "Give me the feathers of the golden eagle." With these in his hands he was able to go as fast as the giant himself. And in a little while they came to the shore of the western sea and found the giant's canoe.

The man said: "Is that a mountain across the sea, with something on the side of it that glitters like snow?"

The giant said: "That is the Great Bear of the West and the thing that glitters on it is the belt of wampum."

The giant launched his canoe and, putting the man in the middle, paddled westward. The canoe shot over the water as fast as they had crossed the land, and soon they were nearing the western shore. There sat the great bear girdled with the belt of wampum. The bear was not like the skunk. He sat motionless by the sea, his ears hanging down and not a hair stirring. His eyes were open but he seemed to be in a stupor.

The giant told the man what they must do when they got ashore, and then they landed and approached the bear. The belt went around his chest, over his left shoulder and under his right leg. The giant was so tall that he could reach clear up and draw the belt over the bear's head, while the man held up the bear's right paw. So they quickly pulled it off and made for the canoe. The giant paddled away at tremendous speed, while the man kept watch on the bear. For a time the bear did not stir.

Then he came slowly down to the shore and he began to draw the sea into his mouth. So strong was the rush of water flowing into his mouth that the giant could not make head[way] against it; in spite of all he could do, the canoe was drawn towards the bear. As it reached him, the giant seized his war club and, standing up, struck the bear with all his might on the forehead.

At that, the giant and the man fell senseless. The man was first to come to himself. The bear was sitting on the shore, but the wampum was still in the canoe. When the giant came to, they started again, and this time they recrossed the sea in safety, for the bear did not move. Then they returned to the man's camp and greeted the woman.

Charles Kawbawgam with stepchild, ca. 1880.

"The most precious wampum in the world," said the giant, "must remain in the north." And giving the man his bag of feathers, he departed homeward.

The Great Skunk and the Great Bear of the West

Homer H. Kidder

On finishing the tale of the Great Skunk and of the Great Bear of the West, Kawbawgam said: "These things must have happened before the Flood, for although the bones of monstrous animals are sometimes found in the ground, no one knows when these animals lived and there are now no more of them in the world."

In other words, if they had lived after the Flood, they would naturally have left descendants of similar size.

I (H.H.K.) answered that I knew it was true as he said, that once there had been monstrous animals in the world and I mentioned that their bones had been discovered by scientists.

On hearing this, as interpreted by Jacques LePique, Kawbawgam smiled and said with his usual gentleness but with fine scorn: "The scientist thinks he understand[s] these things, but the man who knows is the Jessakid"—the Indian soothsayer.

Nothing that Kawbawgam ever said tickled me so much as this, for it proved his unquestioning faith in the ancient lore of his people and in the stories that he was relating.[80]

---

[80] The themes of the two separate Ojibwa tales, "The Great Skunk" and "The Great Bear of the West," are found in one Ottawa myth in which a sleeping bear, in the north, pursues ten brothers who have stolen the wampum but is at length stunned by the magic power of a great Jessakkiwin's bodiless head and is cut into pieces which immediately turn into bears of ordinary size. See Schoolcraft, "Algic Researches" [M. L. Williams 1957: 46–57].

Wampum Hair

Jacques LePique

There was a young man whose hair was of shining white wampum, so thick and long that it covered his back. He lived alone, having little to do with people because he was so proud.

One day a young hunter stopped at his camp. The two sat down by the fire and when they had smoked, the hunter looked around him and said, "My friend, you seem to have everything here."

"Oh, yes," said Wampum Hair. "I have everything I need."

"Still," said the hunter, "there is one thing that you have not got. It seems too bad that a young man like you should be living alone. Why don't you take a wife?"

Wampum Hair said, "Well, I'll tell you. It's because I never saw a woman that was handsome enough or had fine enough hair."

"But I have," said the other. "I've lately seen a girl that is [more] handsome than you, and her hair is as beautiful as yours."

Wampum Hair wanted to know where he had seen her.

"I saw her," answered his friend,

on the top of a mountain, where she lives. That day I was in the form of a bird and flew a long way over the woods till I came to the Whitestone Mountains. On the highest peak are three big pines, and when I came nearer, I saw a huge nest—larger than an eagle's nest—swung between the pines, and a red string hanging down from the nest into the top of a wigwam beneath. I flew up to look, and there, in the nest, lay a beautiful girl. Her eyes were as bright as the stars and her hair covered her body like a shining robe. I could not stir till she put out her hand to touch me on the edge of the nest; and then I flew away. When I got home in my own shape that night, my mother said, "What makes you so quiet my son? Have you seen some girl that you like?" So I told her about the girl in the nest. "And don't you know who that is?" said my mother. "They say she's [the] most beautiful woman in the world. It seems she must stay in that nest for seven years unless some man shall win her. And I think, my friend, that girl would be good enough for you, if you could get her."

Said Wampum Hair: "Will you show me where she lives?"

His friend undertook to guide him and the two young men started the next morning and walked all day. At night they camped by a stream and next day went on through the woods. In the afternoon, as they were nearing the Whitestone Mountains, they saw sunlight under the branches ahead and soon came out on a meadow. In the middle of it stood a round-topped wigwam with smoke coming from it. As the young men drew near, a voice inside said: "Boju, my grandsons." Then they saw an old bent woman coming from the lodge. It was the Mole Woman; sometimes she looked like a mole and sometimes she looked like a woman. She asked which of them had come to seek the young woman, and then she took Wampum Hair into her lodge and said she would help him.

She said that first he must go up the mountain and talk with the young woman's father. "But do not stay long," said she. "Come away soon, and tell me what he says."

So Wampum Hair took the path up the mountain. At the top, he saw the great nest between the three pines and a red string hanging from the nest into a hole in the wigwam. An old man at the door asked him in and when they had smoked, the old man pulled the string, and soon a young woman came into the lodge and sat down at one side. Wampum Hair had never seen such a beautiful woman.

"Well," said the old man, "how do you find the hunting?"

"I have just come to this part of the country," answered Wampum Hair. "How do you find it?"

"Very poor," said the old man. "Now-a-days I never get the kinds of game that I like best."

"And what kinds are those?" Wampum Hair asked.

"The beaver, the white bear, and the elk," said the old man. "Of all meats, I like those three the best."

On hearing this, Wampum Hair got up and went back to the camp of the Mole Woman.

She said, "Do you know why he told you that he likes the meat of these three animals? Because they are the largest and fiercest in the world, and he wants to find out whether you are man enough to kill them. They have killed all the others who have come to win his daughter. But I will help you. Go across the meadow behind this lodge. There, on the stream, is a beaver dam; and you will see the chief of the beavers sitting on the dam. Take this club. If you can get near enough to strike him down, tie this string around his neck, and drag him here."

In those days, the beaver was not a small animal such as he is now. He was many times as big and very fierce. Wampum Hair crawled through the rushes and there saw the chief of the beavers sitting on the dam, watching the other beavers at work in the pond. Wampum Hair leaped on the dam with his club and struck the beaver on the head. The beaver rolled down on the meadow and at the same time Wampum Hair heard the other beavers slapping their tails on the water. He slipped the cord around the neck of the chief and dragged him towards the camp. Then he heard the whole tribe of beavers coming in pursuit and he saw that they were fast overtaking him. He cried out: "I wish I were in the lodge of my grandmother, the Mole Woman." And there he was, with the chief of the beavers lying at the door.

The Mole Woman gave him a comb and a birch bark box, and while she was working on the carcass of the beaver, she told him to comb his hair and put the combings of Wampum into the box. First she drained the beaver's blood, and taking out the heart, lungs, guts, kidneys, and liver, cooked these in the blood for supper and breakfast.

In the morning, Wampum Hair carried the beaver up the mountain and, when he dropped the body it shook the mountain. The old man came out and saw the chief of the beavers lying dead. Then Wampum Hair returned to the Mole Woman.

She said, "Now you must go to hunt the white bear, who lives far in the north. On foot it would take you three years. But you shall be there in a moment. Get ready!"

She gave him a bow and arrows and told him that, when he reached the North, he would see three white bears and must shoot the largest. On her lap lay a buckskin bag, the mouth of it drawn up with gathering strings. Thrusting in her forefingers, she pulled it open, pointing one end at the North. At that instant, Wampum Hair found himself standing amid snow and ice. And not far away he saw three immense white bears coming towards him. Wampum Hair hid behind an iceberg, and when the first bear came in sight, shot him through the heart. Then he quickly tied the magic cord about the bear's neck and dragged him southward. At the same time, he heard the other bears coming with terrible yells, and soon they were at his heels. He cried: "I wish I were in the lodge of my grandmother, the Mole Woman." And there he was, with the great white bear; and he saw that the Mole Woman had drawn the strings of her bag.

While she was bleeding the bear and cooking the guts in the blood, she told Wampum Hair again to comb his hair with the comb she had given him and to put the combings into the birch bark box. At sunrise he carried the white bear up the mountain to the old man and again hurried back to the camp of the Mole Woman.

She said that now he was to go for the chief of the elks, a long journey to the west. But pulling open her buckskin bag, with one hand pointing at the West, she sent him in a moment to the country of the elk. There he killed the chief of the elks and dragged him eastward with the magic cord; and being pursued by the other elks, he cried out as before, and at once he was safe in the camp of the Mole Woman, with the body of the great elk. Again she told him to comb his hair and put the combings into the birch bark box, while she bled the carcass and cooked meat for supper and breakfast in the blood.

At daybreak she told Wampum Hair to take the elk up to the old man. The Mole Woman said to him: "My grandson, you will see me no more. The old man will give you his daughter to be your wife."

So Wampum Hair left her and carried the elk up the mountain and when it fell at the door of the lodge, the mountain trembled. The old man came out with his daughter and said: "You have killed the beaver, the white bear, and the elk. Therefore I know that you are a strong man, able to provide for a family. I thank you for these presents and in return I give the best that I have."

So saying, he led his daughter to Wampum Hair and gave her to him to be his wife; and Wampum Hair took her and they went away.

In the spring Wampum Hair's wife bore a son. The child's hair, like the father's, was of wampum, and at its birth a cradle board of wampum was found beside the mother. But how it came they never knew.

One day when Wampum Hair had gone hunting, the mother went to the brook for water, leaving the child asleep on his cradle board, watched by a little dog. Hearing the dog bark, she ran back. The baby, with his cradle board, and the dog were gone from the lodge. As she ran out, Wampum Hair returned, and when they could nowhere find the child, he said: "Woman, I know now why you were lying in that nest on the mountain. You were fasting for power from the Mishi Ginabig and you promised him your first child. It is Mishi Ginabig that has taken my son."

He tore off her clothes and, driving her out, called the Thunderbirds to take vengeance upon her. The Thunderbirds were sailing over the woods; now and then lightning flashed from their eyes. But the Thunderbirds did not harm her. They dropped a cloak on her to cover her.

Then she went back and found that Wampum Hair had burned the lodge and was gone. But her fear was for her child. Searching all around, she saw the footprints of an enormous frog and with them, the tracks of the little dog, as if he had been dragged along on his paws. She knew then that it was the Frog Woman that had stolen her baby and knew by the tracks that the little dog had tried to hold back the cradle board with his teeth.

The tracks came to an end at the foot of a big tree. She burned the tree and found that it was hollow, and that a hole opened downwards through the roots. Down she went into the hole till she came to the lower world. There again she found the tracks and she followed them for days and for months and for years, hoping always to overtake the Frog Woman and get back her son.

One day she saw the foot prints of a child and she said: "My son can walk." In course of time she found a little bow, and she said: "My son can shoot." Each year she found a larger bow till at length she found a war bow, and she said: "My son is a man."

At last the Frog Woman and Wampum Hair's son reached the end of the lower world and went into camp. Soon the mother came up on their trail and keeping watch, saw the Frog Woman go alone to the cliff that ends the lower world. There she saw the Frog Woman draw the cradle board from her pack and hang it secretly over the edge of the cliff.

All these years the mother had not changed or grown older; she was as beautiful as when she lived in the nest on the mountain. The next day her son, while hunting, was led to her camp by the smell of smoke, and coming suddenly upon her, stopped in surprise. She asked him to sit by her fire, and when they had talked together, she knew that he was falling in love with her. Then she told him that she was his mother, told him of his father, Wampum Hair, told how the Frog Woman had stolen him from her when he was a baby, and that all his life she had followed them.

Wampum Hair's son said: "I have always called this old Frog Woman my mother. You seem to be no older than I. How can I believe that you are my mother?"

"Fetch the little dog," she said. "You will see if he knows me."

So he went back to bring the dog. The little dog ran to her whimpering, leaping up to lick her face.

Then she told him of the cradle board of wampum found at his birth and how, when he was stolen, she knew by the tracks that the little dog had tried to save him by holding back on the cradle board with his teeth.

"The Frog Woman," said she, "has kept the cradle board hidden from you. But if you could get her to show it to you, I think you would see the scratches of the dog's teeth."

So he returned to the Frog Woman and lay down, pretending he was sick.

106

Wampum Hair

The Frog Woman said: "What is the matter with you, my son? What can I do to make you well?"

He said: "It would make me well if I could see my cradle board."

The Frog Woman grew angry. She said: "You know very well that there is no cradle board here."

The young man said no more. For seven days, he lay on one side, and then turning, lay for seven days on the other side always groaning.

At last, fearing that he was going to die, the Frog Woman ran out and brought in the cradle board. Wampum Hair's son took it, saw that it was made of wampum, and saw the marks of the dog's teeth upon it. Then he got up and told her that he was cured. The next morning, the young man started at daybreak and, walking till the sun was overhead, killed a deer and hung it in a tree above the reach of wolves, then he pulled the bark from the trunk so that the tree could easily be spotted. He reached camp at sunset and told the Frog Woman where he had hung the deer, bidding her to fetch it to camp the next day.

As soon as she had started, early in the morning, he took the cradle board and the dog and went to his mother. He said that he knew now that she was in truth his mother and that he had come to take her back to the world above.

"The Frog Woman," said he, "has far to go to carry the deer; but she goes very fast. We must hurry."

So they broke camp and started. But before they had gone far, they heard the Frog Woman coming after them, shrieking with rage. She had turned into a gigantic frog and they saw her coming with great leaps.

"Wait!" shouted Wampum Hair's son. "Do not be afraid, Mother. I will stop that devil of a frog."

He pulled from his belt a long wooden knife and, drawing the point of it across their path, opened a gap in the ground just as the Frog Woman rose for another leap. Down she plunged into the gap and the young man, with one sweep of his wooden knife, closed the ground above her. So the Frog Woman was swallowed up.

Wampum Hair's son found a way back to the upper world and camped with his mother.

He said: "I will take care of you always. But first I have something to do. I am going to find my father."

Taking his war bow, he went away and was gone many days. When he returned, he carried at his belt a scalp of white wampum. He had avenged his mother.[81]

---

[81] See Schoolcraft, "Hiawatha or Manabozho" in *The Hiawatha Legends* [1856:29]. "He appeared to be rejoiced to hear that his father was living, for he had already thought in his heart to try and kill him."

The Girls and the Porcupine

Kawbawgam

The girls started out to set traps on a fine day in winter. As they went along they saw a porcupine. The older girl said: "Let's take that porcupine and pull out his quills so that he will freeze." The other said: "No, no! Don't do such a thing." But the older girl caught the porcupine and plucked out most of his quills and bristles, leaving only a tuft of hair on his head and one on each paw, then she let him go and the porcupine climbed a tree. When he got to the top, he faced towards the north and sang to Ka-bi-bo-na-kay (the north wind) asking him to send the greatest snow storm ever known. While he was singing, the girls went on to set their traps. Soon it began to blow from the north, terribly cold, with driving snow. The girls were frightened and started home, but in the blinding snow they lost their way and wandered apart. The younger girl at last reached camp, worn out and with frozen hands, but the girl who had tortured the porcupine was never seen again.[82]

---

[82] Kawbawgam says he doesn't believe that this really happened but that the tale was invented by some storyteller who wanted to teach a lesson, namely, that no one should be cruel to animals. See the story of "The Man from the World Above" [p. 85] concerning waste and game.

Chickadee Boy

Kawbawgam

This is the story of a very little boy, the smallest in all the nations of men. He had a bow and arrows, and when he killed a chickadee his sister made him a coat of the skin.

The boy lived with his sister on the shore of a large lake. Their father and their mother and the people of the camps near by had, one after another, been killed by two evil spirits in the form of bears. The girl did not know what had become of their parents and she was always in fear for herself and her brother.

Once the boy said: "Sister, why are there only two of us on this earth?" She answered: "We are the only ones in this part of the earth."

For he was so bold she was afraid that if she told him that there might be other people living on the shores of the lake, he would go looking for them and that he too might be lost or killed in the woods. So she told him that he must never go far from camp.

But each day Chickadee Boy went a little farther than the day before, and one afternoon he ran across a beaten path. He said to himself: "Someone has made this trail." He meant to find out who it could be, and the next morning he took his bow, and going back to the trail, followed it through the woods till it led him into a cave under a hill. As he came along, two monstrous bears, one red, the other black, came out at him from the cave. Chickadee Boy strung his bow, and before the bears could get to him, he shot and killed them both.

These bears were the spirits that had killed their neighbors. Of all who had met them only Chickadee Boy had the power to overcome them. But whether his power was given him by the chickadee or by some other spirit, the story-teller is in the dark.

On the belly of each bear, Chickadee Boy saw a lump under the skin, and cutting these lumps open, he took from each a bunch of human hair. One was the hair of his father and the other was the hair of his mother. He could not remember his parents yet he knew their hair. He knew that the bears had killed them, and he began to mourn for them, and cried all the way home. His sister ran out to meet him, and asked him why he was crying. So he showed her the hair and told her he had slain the spirit bears that had killed their mother and father.

Chickadee Boy often played on the shore and his sister said: "If your arrow should fall on the lake, do not go after it, for a fish might get you." This gave him an idea. And one evening he threw off his chickadee coat on the beach, waded into the water, and called out: "Big fish with the red fins, come swallow me." His sister looked out and saw a big fish come up and take him. But first he shouted to her: "Tie something to a string and throw it on the water." The girl made a line of basswood bark and fastening one end to a tree, tied the other end to an old moccasin and threw this into the lake. In the night, the fish swam near the moccasin. The boy said: "Bite." And the fish took hold of it and held on. In the morning, the girl found the line stretched taught, and pulling in the fish, she opened him with her knife and thumb. Out jumped Chickadee Boy, and said: "I've been fishing, sister. Wash me off."

When winter set in and the lake froze over, Chickadee Boy asked his sister to make him a wooden ball and a stick curved at the end. With his stick he would drive his ball along the ice; it flew like the wind, but however fast it went, the boy followed just as fast. He was always right behind it, as if the ball gave him its speed.

One day, having knocked his ball to the far end of the lake, he saw nine black shapes on the ice, and going towards them, he found they were young giants, fishing through holes cut in the ice. As he came up, he wished that the nearest giant would see a fish. At the same moment, the giant saw one, but as he jabbed with his spear, the boy knocked his ball into the hole; so that the giant missed his mark. The giant sang out: "Look at this little man"; and all the giants laughed. They thought he was comical and gave him back his ball. But as soon as they began to watch their holes again, Chickadee Boy tied a string to a fish that lay on the ice and ran away with it. A giant said: "See that boy go!" And in a moment he was out of sight.

When the giants went home, they told the other giants about this, and an old woman said, "Don't touch that boy. He is a spirit. Give him anything he wants." The next day Chickadee Boy came again and took another fish, and the day after that still another. The fourth time he came, he again knocked his ball into a hole so that another giant lost a fish. Then he asked for his ball but the giant would not give it to him.

The others said: "Let him have it."

But the giant said: "Are we going to be ruled by a little boy like this?"

As the giant stooped to pick up the ball, the boy struck him with his stick and broke the giant's arm. The ball rolled on the ice and Chickadee Boy, seizing another fish, gave the ball a rap with his stick, and sped away down the lake.

The giants went home very angry. The old woman said: "Never mind what he does. You'd better leave him alone." But they would not listen to her, and the next morning they set out to kill him.

Now Chickadee Boy always ate the eye of his game and his dish was a clam shell. In the morning his sister cooked the fish and had just put an eye into his shell when they heard the ice crack with a loud boom. The girl ran out to the beach and saw nine giants coming down the lake. She begged her brother to flee, but Chickadee Boy sat where he was, eating the eye of his fish. By the time he had swallowed the last mouthful, the giants had come right in front of the camp, running towards the shore. The boy turned his clam shell upside-down; the ice went to pieces and the giants were all drowned.

The League of the Four Upper Algonquian Nations

Kawbawgam

After the Flood the descendants of the first father and mother spread all over the country. Then began countless wars. Many peoples fought the Ojibwas, [and] seemed to have a spite against them. But after many years four tribes came together in peace to hold a council. These tribes were the Ojibwas, the Ottawas, the Potawatomies, and the Menominees.[83]

I believe that this meeting was held at the Sault Ste. Marie in the times of my father's grandfather. The pipe and the belt of wampum used in that council are still at the Sault in the keeping of my brother Wabememe, chief by the English treaty. The belt is decorated with a stripe of white beads which runs all around the middle and is called the Road of Peace. The edges outside of the white stripe are colored. The meaning of the pipe and also of the belt of wampum was that these were a pledge of everlasting peace and bound the brothers to help anyone of them that might be in trouble, for by this treaty the four tribes made an eternal brotherhood. The oldest brothers were the Ojibwas, next the Ottawas, next the Potawatomies, and the youngest brothers were the Menominees. The last council that these tribes held was in 1855 at Manitou Island on the Canadian side of the Saint Mary's River. There were several thousand Indians in that council. My stepfather, Shaweno,[84] was head chief of the Ojibwas. My father, Black Cloud (Muk-kud-day-wuk-kwud), was another chief, and I was an underchief.

The four nations were assembled to settle trouble that came up

---

[83] The Menominees, as a smaller tribe, were not always mentioned among the Algonquian tribes commonly known, in the eighteenth century as "The Three Fires."

[84] In regard to Kawbawgam's stepfather, Shaweno, it seems [that] Kawbawgam's mother had a second husband while her first was still alive.

through the Menominees. A Menominee was thought to have disappeared, the year before, in the Red River country, and the council was called to take steps to find him. His sister had said that he was away on a buffalo hunt on the prairies, but this the Menominees did not believe. They said that the man must be found and accused the Ojibwas of killing him. The Menominees were so angry that they were ready to break the brotherhood and go to war against the Ojibwas.

The Ottawa orator rose and spoke in favor of the Ojibwas and told the Menominees that "the Ojibwa whip was not easy to break." The Potawatomie orator also spoke in favor of the Ojibwas and said that the Menominees, being the youngest of the brotherhood, should therefore be reasonable, and advised them "not to risk breaking their long friendship with the Ojibwas." Finally the four tribes made a new treaty of peace.

The following spring the lost Menominee who was the cause of the trouble, came back from the Red River.

Fight with the Iroquois[85]

Kawbawgam

A great war party of Iroquois came up from the lower lakes. As they
paddled along the shore of Georgian bay, the Ojibwas in that neighborhood pushed on ahead of them and gave warning of their approach.
The Ojibwas traveled day and night to the Sault, gathering numbers as
they went, till they reached Lake Superior and felt able to fight. They
then camped secretly at Point aux Pins, while the Iroquois passed them
the next day and camped on the other side of the water at Iroquois Point.
As they went along, not knowing that they were watched, the Iroquois
began to sing their war songs, and when they landed they had a war
dance.

The Ojibwa chief called for two strong medicine men to go scout-
ing. The scouts were unarmed for they were to go in spirit form. Presently the Ojibwas waiting on the beach, heard a beaver in the water and
heard the whistle of an otter. These were the two medicine men. They
swam across the bay going ashore between Whiskey Bay [and] Iroquois
Point, and resumed their own forms. They went through the woods
towards the other point and as soon as it was dark, crept up and counted
the Iroquois. Then they went back to their landing place, recrossed the

---

[85] *Editor's Note:* This famous battle at Iroquois Point, presently in Chippewa County, Michigan, is given in numerous versions, beginning with the *Jesuit Relations,* where this victory
of 1662 is ascribed to the Sauteurs over a war party of Mohawks and Oneidas (Thwaites
1896–1901:4, 10) . Perrot's account, written before 1718, honors bands of Ojibwa, Ottawa,
Nipissing, and Amikoue over undifferentiated Iroquois (1864:179–182). Alexander Henry's account of 1776 gives a thousand Iroquois defeated by three hundred Chippewa with
but a single casualty and that due to a stabbing with an awl by an old woman (1809:193–
194). McKenney's version has an alliance of Chippewa and Fox crossing over the ice in
winter (1827:214), while in Warren's account Ojibwa defeat Iroquois weakened by carous-
ing and inebriation (1852:147–148).

bay in animal form, and returned to camp, arriving about dawn. They knew from a spirit that the Iroquois would continue their dance all day and night for four days. And the Ojibwa chief understood that by that time they would be all tired out.

Most Iroquois war parties carry along one woman. The squaw with this party dreamed every night that the Iroquois were all going to be killed by the Ojibwas. She told the Iroquois chief but he thought nothing of it.

In the morning that the medicine men came back to Point aux Pins, the Ojibwas moved across to Whiskey Bay to wait till it was time to attack.

On the fourth day they sent two more scouts to find out when the Iroquois were going to sleep. About the same time, the whole band of Ojibwas began to move through the woods towards the enemy camp. Meantime the scouts were working back and forth and reported at last that all the Iroquois seemed to be asleep.

The Ojibwas gradually drew up and surrounded them till the scouts had only a little way to go to take their reports to the chief. Near dawn he ordered the men to attack. The Iroquois, tired out after their long war dance, were taken entirely by surprise. They were slaughtered in heaps. Only two were spared. The Ojibwas took these two, cut off their ears, noses, fingers and toes, gave them supplies enough to get home and sent back this message: That that party of Iroquois wasn't big enough to give the Ojibwas a little fun and that if anymore felt like coming, they could count upon getting the same welcome. The Ojibwas cut off the heads of the slain and set them up, one after another, along the beach in a line that stretched about half a mile.

Kawbawgam's grandmother as a very old woman when once gathering firewood on the beach, picked up some arm and leg bones of Iroquois killed in that fight, mistaking them, as her sight was dim, for sticks of wood.

Two Stories of Sauks Head

Jacques LePique and Charlotte Kawbawgam

VERSION I

Probably more than a hundred years ago, an Ojibwa named Yellow Dog was going up Lake Superior with his wife and two children, a boy of sixteen or seventeen and a baby. The boy was paddling with his father. They camped that evening after passing Shot Point,[86] and in the morning went on in a thick fog.

That same morning a small war party of Sauks arrived on Lake Superior having crossed from Lake Michigan on a trail that comes out of the woods at the mouth of the Chocolay. Near there, they climbed a high rock to get a view of the shore; but as there was a heavy fog, they could see nothing. Presently, however, out on [the] water they heard a baby crying, and listening how the sound moved, they knew that some Ojibwas must be passing up the coast.

This was Yellow Dog's party heading across Iron Bay towards Presque Isle, on their way along the shore. A couple of days later, they arrived at the mouth of a river where they were going to camp.

It seems that Yellow Dog's son, who had some medicine power and could see into the future a little, told his father that he was anxious. Old Yellow Dog evidently didn't pay much attention when his son said that some danger was approaching, though from what direction, he could not tell. The young man was uneasy all night and was up at dawn on the watch. When he went to the mouth of the river, a few steps away, he saw a light band of fog still stretched along the water from the point

---

[86] The English name says Jacques LePique, came from the loss of a bag of shot by some men who stopped on their way along the lake; and when one of them returned, some time afterwards, he found the bag broken and the shot spread on the ground. *Editor's Note:* Footnote appears as an addendum to the listing of Shot Point in "Some Ojibwa Place Names" in the Kidder manuscript and has been transposed here as its first mention in the present text.

on the east, and he saw several dark objects which he couldn't quite make out.

"It may be some enemy," he said to himself. And he called his father who then came out to look.

"No, no," said Yellow Dog. "That's nothing to be afraid of. Some gulls on a log."

At that, they returned to camp; but the boy couldn't sit still. Taking his father's gun he went to look once more. And this time, hardly a paddle's length from the beach, he saw two canoes full of Sauks. They jumped ashore and ran after him. He rushed past the camp, calling his father to flee, and at the same time wheeled about, fired, and killed two Sauks at a shot. Then he plunged into a thicket and lay concealed. There he heard the death cries of his family and soon afterwards saw the lodge go up in flames.

The Sauks carried their dead companions to the beach and laid them, one in each canoe. They blackened their faces and bodies with charcoal, in sign of mourning, and then pushed off in the direction from which they had come.

All this the young man saw from his hiding place. He had now made up his mind to follow and take revenge. He set out under cover of the woods, and [the] Sauks paddled so slowly, singing their death chant to a measured stroke, that he was able to keep abreast of them, although he had to follow the bends of the shore. About ten miles below, they stopped at a small island a good stone's throw from the mainland. Here he saw them lift the dead men from the canoes and bury them in a rift in the rocks. This done, they washed off the charcoal, got into the canoes again, and paddled swiftly away down the coast.

When they were out of sight beyond the next point, the young man swam across to the island. He dug up the two bodies, cut off their heads and stuck these on the low stub-branches of some pines that stand in a grove on the inner side of the island.

There after the Ojibwas called that place, "The island where the Sauks heads hang," and the stream that flows into the lake some ten miles further west they called, "The river where Yellow Dog was killed."

So, according to the story just told, the neighboring promontory of Sauks Head takes its name from the island, and the word "head" refers not, as one might suppose to the promontory, but to the heads of the two Sauks that were dug up by Yellow Dog's son.

From Charlotte Kawbawgam's story, which follows, one would infer that the name belonged to the point itself. Which possibly it does. But that seems very likely to remain a question. Be that as it may, here is the tale that was told to Charlotte by her father Matji-gijig.

117

OJIBWA NARRATIVES

A large war party of Sauks came north from Lake Michigan. Passing the Straits of Mackinaw, they paddled up the St. Mary's River and thence went along the south shore of Lake Superior. By the time they reached Iron Bay, the Ojibwas of that region sent messengers to muster fighters. These were to meet near the point that has since been known as Sauks Head, for one of the medicine men in the council, a man in whom the people had great confidence, had told the Chiefs that the Sauks would make a nights camp at that point. This medicine man prayed to his spirit for a heavy fog that the Ojibwas might come together without being seen. By afternoon the fog had settled down over the lake, and the Ojibwas collected in the woods west of Sauks Head, where the enemy were going to camp.

The spies sent out at dusk returned in the night to report that the Sauks, after their long day of paddling, had all gone to sleep. A little before dawn the Ojibwas surrounded the Sauk camp, and at a signal from the chief, rushing in, massacred the Sauks to the last man. On the same day the scalps were brandished in a great scalp dance.[87] From that day, the place has been known as Sauks Head.

VERSION II[88]

Looking across the bay [from Marquette], you see between the mouth of the Chocolay River and the State Prison, a tall, bare quartzite knob which most persons familiar with landmarks in this vicinity probably call the "Chippewa Lookout." Obviously, the name connects itself with old Indian warfare. Now it is known that the Chippewas of Eastern Lake Superior lived in a state of hereditary belligerence against the Sacs, Sauks, or Siaks, of Lake Michigan. In a letter on this subject, my friend Mr. William Jones, of Howard College, a Sauk Indian familiar with the traditions of his people, writes, "War parties of each tribe constantly made incursions against the other, going mostly by land and on foot." Of

---

[87] *Editor's Note:* The presence of Sauk Indians on the south shore of Lake Superior is reported by the Jesuit missionary Allouez in 1667 who notes that they are numerous but scattered and wandering (Thwaites 1896–1901:41;45). Although Sauk traditions state a pre-contact home in the Saginaw valley of lower Michigan, the Green Bay region remained their center from 1668 until 1733 when they fled together with the Fox to the lower Wisconsin River and into what is now eastern Iowa. Their role as the opposing ball team and allies of the Ojibwa under Chief Pontiac in taking Fort Mackinaw on June 4, 1763, as well as laying seige to eleven other British stockaded forts, belies traditional animosities implied in this and the following narrative.

[88] *Editor's Note:* Kidder published the second version as "Two Local Indian Traditions," in *The Mining Journal* (Marquette, Michigan), Special Edition, Jan. 1, 1898, 13, and hand copied the article at the end of the manuscript while at Berkeley, California, on November 15, 1942.

the old trails thus and otherwise beaten across the peninsula from Lake Michigan, Green Bay, and that neighborhood, one is said to have come out near the mouth of the Chocolay, and Jack LePique—by whom a story relative to the matter is given below—tells me, that on reaching Lake Superior by this trail, the Sauks used to climb the neighboring rock to scan the shore for their enemies, and that the height in question was known to this tribe not as the Chippewa, but the Sauks' Watch or Lookout, Osaugeeahkawwahbewin.

The recollection of this name by an Indian who knew the coast long before the town of Marquette was thought of, shows pretty conclusively, I think, that our name for the rock is a blunder. In fact, the hill would naturally have been used as a lookout rather by invaders than by natives. If, as appears from Charlotte Kawbawgam's story—also given below—the Sauks came sometimes by way of the St. Mary's River and so along the south shore, it is possible that, in case of alarm, the Chippewas hereabout might themselves station a sentinel on the height to give warning of the approach of canoes from the direction of Grand Island. They did not, however, in the story.

Her legend, as will be seen, is much shorter than Jack LePique's, has less specific detail and in fact, though this is uncertain, may be a decayed version of the same tradition. One cannot help thinking, at any rate, that to surprise this part of the coast, the Sauks, instead of going around through the Straits of Mackinaw, up the St. Mary's—always strewn with Chippewa encampments—and from thence along the open shore, would find it far easier and safer to come directly overland through the woods. That such was the case seems pretty certain, moreover, from Mr. Jones' testimony above. Now to the Chippewas, fearful of attack from the interior, it would probably seem advisable to put scouts in ambush up the trail, rather than on a hill from which it is not possible to look inland more than a short distance. To Sauk invaders, however, nothing could be more natural, on coming from the woods, than to mount some height for a view of the coast. On the whole, therefore, though in the exigencies of that stealthy warfare both Sauks and Chippewa may at odd turns have climbed the rock to spy upon each other, there seems, (so far as origin and common sense are concerned), decidedly better reason to call it "Sauks Lookout" than by the name in use today.

And now for the legends themselves. The following is Jack LePique's:

In ancient times, probably more than a hundred years ago, an old Chippewa named Yellow Dog, was once camped with his wife and two children, near Shot Point. One of these children was a boy of sixteen or seventeen, the other was a baby.

At that time, a small war party of Sauks arrived on Lake Superior, having crossed from the neighborhood of Green Bay, on a trail that comes out of the woods near the Chocolay. They climbed Sauk Lookout for a view of the shore; but as there happened to be a heavy fog on the lake, they could see nothing. Presently, however, they heard a noise out on the water, a baby crying, and noticing how the sound moved, they knew that some Chippewas must be passing up the coast.

It was old Yellow Dog's party [that] had broken camp that morning and were heading across the bay towards Presque Isle, on their way to the Yellow Dog River (a stream which received its name from a subsequent event in this story). They arrived there about sun down and went into camp. The young fellow, who had some medicine power and could see into the future a little, got the idea that they were in great peril. He told his father, but the old man didn't pay much attention to him. The boy, however, insisted that some danger was approaching them, though from what direction he said he could not tell. He slept very uneasily that night, and was up at dawn on the watch. He noticed a narrow band of fog still stretched along the water from the point on the east. At the upper edge of it, he saw several black objects and at the lower edge something that looked like a log.

"Perhaps," he said to himself, "it is an enemy approaching." And he called his father to look.

"No, no," said the old man, "That's nothing to be afraid of. It is only a few gulls on a log." At this they returned to camp; but the boy, unable to sit still, took a gun and went to look once more. This time, sure enough, hardly a paddle's length from the beach, he saw two canoes full of painted Sauks. They jumped ashore and ran after him. He rushed by the camp calling upon his father to escape, and at the same time wheeled about, fired, and killed two Sauk at a shot. Then he plunged into the woods and lay concealed. He heard the death cries of his parents and soon afterwards saw the lodge go up in flames.

The Sauks carried their dead companions to the beach and laid them one in each canoe. They then blackened their faces and bodies with charcoal, as a sign of mourning, and pushed off in the direction from which they had come.

All this the boy saw from his hiding place. He now resolved to follow and take such revenge as he could. So he set out under cover of the woods, and the Sauks paddled so slowly, singing their death-chant, to a measured stroke, that he kept abreast of them though he had to follow the bends of the shore. At last, ten miles below, they stopped on a small island—a good stone's throw from the mainland—just opposite a little point of sandstone. Here the boy saw them lift the dead men from the canoes and bury them in a rift of the rocks. This done, they washed off the charcoal, got into their canoes again, and paddled swiftly away down the coast.

When they were out of sight round the point (Garlic Point), the boy swam across to the island. He dug up the two bodies, cut off the heads, and stuck these on the low stub-branches of some pines that stand in a grove on the inner side of the island.

Thereafter the Chippewas called that place "the island where the Sauks' heads hang," and the stream that flows into the lake ten miles above they called "the river where old Yellow Dog was killed."

This is Jack's tale. In recent years through abbreviation and the corruption of translation into English, the names have become simply "Sauks Head Island" and "The Yellow Dog River." According to this story, therefore, the neighboring promontory of Sauks Head gets its name from the island, and the word "head" refers not, as one would suppose, to the jutting shape of the point, but to the crania, now mentioned only in the singular, of those two unfortunate, if bloody-minded, Sauks.

From Charlotte Kawbawgam's story, which follows, we might be led, however, to conclude that the name was first applied to the point itself; but I confess I am disposed, for reasons already given, to attach more importance to the legend just told:

It appears that a fairly large war party of Sauks came through from the south. They went around by the Straits of Mackinaw, up the St. Mary's, and from thence along the south shore. By the time they got to the Chocolay, the Ojibwas of the neighborhood hearing of their approach, got themselves into safety and sent messengers through the woods to muster a band of warriors. These were to meet near Sauks Head; for one of the medicine men in the council had announced, before the messengers set out, that the Sauks would make a night's camp at that place. This medicine man prayed to his spirit for a heavy fog that the Chippewas might come together unobserved. By afternoon, the fog had settled down over the water and the Chippewas collected secretly in the bay above Sauks Head, the invaders having already gone into camp on the point. The spies that were sent out at dusk came back late in the night to say that all the Sauks had gone to sleep. A little before dawn, the Chippewas surrounded the camp, rushed in on their enemies, killed them all, and cut off their heads. The scalps were afterwards flourished in a great war dance. From this event the place received the name of Sauks Head.

Sauks at Portage Entry

Jacques LePique

A large band of Ojibwas had gathered for the summer at Portage Entry on Keeweenaw Point. One evening two boys from the camp paddled across the bay to spear sturgeon by torch light. It was getting dark as they neared Piquaming [Peguahming], and when they came around on the east side, they saw a large number of fires at the edge of the woods along the beach. The boys drew back at once and paddled back to report what they had seen.

The chief called all the men for a council. They did not know who the people in the camp at Piquaming could be, whether friends or enemies; so a pipe was offered to a medicine man. He accepted it, and after smoking, said that the camp seen by the two boys was a big party of Sauks who had come on the war path and meant to attack them early in the morning.

He said: "I suppose some of you are medicine men. Take the pipe around and get two or three to go over as spies."

Two young men accepted the pipe. They waded into the water and swam across to Piquaming in the dark. By the aid of their spirit they were in the form of beavers.

Meantime the Chief said: "The Sauks will probably strike just before daylight. We must send the women and children up the river to Portage Lake. The fighting men will go up stream to the foot of the lake and get in ambush on both sides of the river. No doubt the Sauks will follow us up stream. But no one must raise the war whoop till you hear me yell."

When the scouts in the form of beavers had swum across to Piquaming, they saw a young woman from the Sauk camp coming down to the beach for water. She had a torch and saw the splash of one of the beavers as he drew back from the beach. The spies watched the Sauks getting their canoes ready and then swam back across the bay to tell the chief.

He heard their report and gave the word to start. He said: "We will leave the wigwams just as they are, so that the Sauks will not know that we have left."

During the night the Ojibwas moved up river and hid their canoes in the woods. In the morning, when the Sauks came by, the Ojibwas shot from ambush and killed every man of them but two. These two, being captured, were sent home to the Sauks country with their ears cut off.

Some Ojibwa History

Kawbawgam

No one knows where the first Ojibwas came from, but a small band somewhere in the Lake Superior country spread out and became the Ojibwa Nation. They fought the Sioux and finally drove them from the shores of Lake Superior.

When the Sioux were driven west of the Mississippi those living nearest the Ojibwas on the west were too [far] to fight them; but the Prairie Sioux used to send war parties against the Ojibwas, and there was fighting back and forth. The Sioux always fight. Long after they were driven from Lake Superior by the Ojibwas, they turned against the white people.

In the war of 1812, when the English found they could not beat the Yankees, they went for help to the Indians, and offered large presents to the Ojibwas at St. Joseph's Island in the St. Mary's River. They called to their aid only the able-bodied men but did not tell the Ojibwas that the object was to fight. The British officer asked the Ojibwas if there were any more men to come, and hearing that there were not, he told the chief that they were to go to Mackinaw, then held by the Americans. There were about fifty British soldiers in the expedition.

They went down the St. Mary's River in canoes, passed Mackinaw Island and going ashore at British Landing, surrounded the American barracks at Mackinaw with artillery and Indians.

The American Captain's wife begged her husband with tears to give up the fort. He wanted to fight but the second time she begged him, he hauled down the flag to save the garrison from being exterminated, for the British had other Indians to aid them besides the Ojibwa and the Americans had no chance against them. So the captain gave up the fort.

Going further back in history, when the French were overcome by the English,[89] the English came in and at first abused the Indians, who then determined to have revenge. The Ojibwas and Fox Indians massacred the English garrison in Fort Mackinaw by their trick in the game of *bagataway.*[90] Later on, the English made a treaty with the Indians, saying that if the Americans came they would steal the land and make slaves of the Indians, while the English would give the Indians presents. Therefore the Ojibwas helped the English.

But afterwards the English stopped sending presents and turned from the Indians. The governor said: "These are the last presents. We give no more."

The Ojibwas then turned to the Yankees and made up their minds not to help the English if they got into trouble again. This was decided about forty years ago when there was a meeting and council on the Island of Manitoulin.

The reason that the Indians do not believe in "papers" is that they learned from these happenings that "papers" cannot be depended on, for the promise signed by the British in the treaty, agreeing to make presents to the Indians "as long as the sun rose and set," was broken.

---

[89] In the war terminated by the treaty of Paris, 1763.

[90] Referring to the ruse by which the Indians surprised the English garrison. See Alexander Henry [1809:85–93] and his account of the massacre. *Editor's Note:* The ballgame was the most popular men's game in the western Great Lakes region for recreation, but it also involved gift exchange and had religious significance. Rand P. Ritzenthaler (1970) presents an excellent overview (see Kidder's note 93).

Wyagaw

Kawbawgam

Wyagaw was chief of a band on Lake Superior. He was also a great medicine man; through fasting he had gained power to command the weather, and could at any time cause rain, calm, or fog.

Wyagaw once led a small war party against the Fox Indians.[91] It happened, at the same time, that the Fox were raising a large war party to go against Wyagaw on Lake Superior, not knowing that he had already started against them. When he approached their country one of their medicine men knew that he was coming, so that canoes were sent out to find him.

Wyagaw's party were then on a river all in one canoe. The Fox had many canoes; and in going along the river, they saw a track of bubbles and foam left by the passing of a canoe. Their medicine man told them it was the track of Wyagaw, and they followed.

By this time, the Ojibwas had got to a swampy island, half full of water and hid themselves in the woods. Here they were soon tracked and surrounded by the Fox. But when Wyagaw saw that they were hemmed in, he called a thick fog and turned himself and his men into saw-billed ducks.[92] In that form they made a dash to get through the enemy in the fog; and when the ducks could not take them fast enough under pursuit, he turned himself and his men into muskalonge. In that form they all reached the mainland; but Wyagaw and one of his men who was lame, were captured, while the rest escaped.

The Fox were glad to take Wyagaw alive because they wanted to learn how he got his wonderful power. They carried him and his companion to their camp, and on the way they kept offering him a medicine rattle

---

[91] Whom the Ojibwas called Outagawmies.

[92] The saw-bill duck is the morganser.

with the hope that he would take it and sing his medicine song, telling how he had gained his power. But Wyagaw refused the rattle till they reached the camp, saying he was a prisoner, about to die and that it was of no use to sing.

The custom of the Fox was to burn their prisoners. They used to stand them on a scaffold, wrapped in birch bark, bound hand and foot to heavy crutches that rose above the platform.

Before putting Wyagaw on the scaffold, they offered him the medicine rattle once more. Suddenly he made up his mind to take it. He said that his power was from thunder itself and he began to sing his song. When he had thus got his power into his hands; he climbed the scaffold. All at once the sky turned black; it was so dark the people looking on could hardly see each other. The scaffold broke down with a crash. Rain fell in torrents, the lightning flashed, and it thundered terribly. The Fox were filled with dread and begged Wyagaw to calm the storm. After a while it began to clear and slowly became fine again.

The Fox decided to send Wyagaw homeward with an escort of ten or twelve men. These went only half way with him, being afraid of the Ojibwas. But after that the Fox troubled him no more. Wyagaw was long remembered by this story and also by others about him.

In one story, while Wyagaw was looking around in the woods one day, he noticed an enormous red willow. You know that the red willow seldom grows more than two or three fingers thick, so Wyagaw was much surprised at the size of this one. He took his knife and bored a hole through the bark to see how thick it was. This took a good while. He was getting through towards the wood when he saw a giant mosquito sitting on a tree close by.

Sagimay, the mosquito, thought, "I will taste him."

Wyagaw thought: "Do not bite me. If you do, it will kill me."

The mosquito had a bill as long as a spike. But Wyagaw's thought was so powerful that the mosquito could not bite him. When Wyagaw went back to camp, he dried the bark that he had bored from the red willow, and he told the people about this tree and about the giant mosquito.

One day, late in the winter Wyagaw was out hunting—for bear, porcupine, or any kind of game—when he heard his dogs barking. He wondered what they were barking at. Suddenly the barking ceased. Wyagaw went ahead and soon found his dogs lying as if dead on the snow.

He said: "What has happened to my dogs?"

When he came up, he saw two strange looking animals on a tree. Although Wyagaw had such power, yet as soon as his eyes met theirs, he became so sleepy that he fell down by his dogs on the crust of the snow.

After a while he awoke and shot the two strange animals. They looked like a cross between a porcupine and a raccoon. He didn't know what they were, but it seems that in those days they were called *weenqwuk* a kind of being between a spirit and an animal. They could make anything, whether beast or man, go to sleep. They were not so big but that Wyagaw could carry them both home when his dogs woke up.

As he approached the camp, the men were playing bagataway[93] and the woman were playing pa-pa-sa-ka-way-win.[94] They stopped playing and ran towards Wyagaw to see what he had. But before they got to him, they all fell down on the snow, one after another, sound asleep.[95]

---

[93] Bagataway was, I understand, the game from which the Canadians developed Lacrosse. It is described in Alexander Henry (1809:9, 77–78). *Editor's Note: pagaadowewin,* Indian ball play (Baraga 1878:I, 22)

[94] Pa-pa-sa-ka-way-win was played by two opposing parties of women. Two small balls, tied together by a string a few inches long, was tossed through the air by means of a stick in the hands of each player, the object being to throw the balls past the goal of the opposing party.

[95] Laughing on the part of Kawbawgam and Jacques le Pique [See Schoolcraft (1856:207–208), "Weeng, the spirit of sleep."].

Our Brother-in-Law's Adventures

Kawbawgam

When Kitchi Nonan[96] came from the old country, he lived at the Sault, and the Ojibwas married him to a girl named Kitchi Agenayquay[97]. So he had brothers-in-law and they used [to] make up stories about him, as the Indians often do about their brothers-in-law.[98]

One was a story about a hunting trip that he made with these brothers-in-law and his wife. They camped beside a lake, and that night, while they were sitting around the fire, some geese lighted on the water close by. They could hear the geese squawking and were sorry that they couldn't shoot them because it was dark.

Kitchi Agenayquay said: "Why don't you shoot anyway? You might hit one of them."

Kitchi Nonan did so—banged off his gun and came back to the fire. In the morning, the brothers went down to the water to look. They found a tree shot through, then a rabbit lying dead in the line of the shot. Before the shot had reached the geese a muskrat had got a dose of it. Then the shot killed four or five ducks and also a sucker that happened to jump out of the water. Quite a selection for bouillon!

One day Kitchi Nonan started out for beaver. He had a bow and arrows, and as he went along he shot at a deer. The arrow went through the deer, then through a partridge and passing on, killed first a bear that was reaching up for acorns and then a porcupine at the foot of the oak.

---

[96] That is, Great or Wise Nolin. This was Jacques LePique's grandfather, Louis Nolin, the older, an Irish boy left an orphan in France, where he was adopted by a childless French couple who bequeathed their money to him. He immigrated to Canada and settled at the Sault Ste. Marie (see p. 139).

[97] That is, Big Angeline, Jacques' grandmother.

[98] The relation of brothers-in-law seems to have been one of bantering good fellowship. Apparently brothers-in-law were a subject of jokes in much the same way that mothers-in-law are with us.

Then the arrow stuck in the tree. It was his brothers-in-law who told all this.

Another day Nonan started off through the woods with his gun on his shoulder and came to a lake full of ducks. Hoping to kill a large number of them but having only one charge, he bent his gun between the trunks of a double tree so that it would shoot in a curve, and so killed all of the ducks with one shot.

In the spring, Kitchi Nonan took a walk to another lake, and there he saw several swans. Wanting to catch them but not knowing how in the world to do it, he finally dove under the water and swam around till he found where the swans were; then tied all their feet together with a line and gave it a jerk. Away went the swans through the air, with Kitchi Nonan hanging on to the line. After being carried for miles, he lost his hold and fell.[99] As luck would have it, he landed right in the top of a hollow pine just as a bear was coming out. Nonan tumbled on the bear and surprised it so it scrambled out of the tree and ran away.

The next time that Kitchi Nonan went hunting was in winter. Coming onto the tracks of some moose, he put after them to run them down. He ran nearly all day. He was so excited he hardly knew what he was doing. Something seemed to be hanging onto him, holding him back, but he didn't have time to stop and find out what it was. At last, when he overtook and killed one of the moose, he then found that a deer, which he had forgotten, was tied on his back.

When Nonan got older he bought a piece of land where the fort is now, and built a trading post there. Then he gave up hunting and took to buying furs.

One day, early in the fall, while smoking at his door, he caught sight of a flock of geese flying so high that he could barely see them. He rushed for his gun and shot, though he thought they were a good deal too high to hit. A little later, a goose fell down the chimney!

The Indians thought that Kitchi Nonan had more than human wisdom. He seemed to know about almost everything. The Indians used to go to his trading post to hear him talk. They would sit down, light their pipes and listen. He became a great man among them, and after his death these stories that had been told by his brothers-in-law, came to be known by nearly everyone.[100]

---

[99] *Editor's Note:* This episode is a well known Nanabozho theme. See Skinner and Satterlee (1915:267).

[100] The form of these yarns, as told by Kawbawgam, largely disappears in taking them down as interpreted. Kawbawgam more or less acted out each episode and the Indians present were once or twice convulsed with laughter, as for example, when he showed how Kitchi Nonan bent the barrel of his gun to make it shoot in a curve, and so killed all the ducks with a single charge. The story of the brothers-in-law and their adventures reminds one of "Iagoo" in Schoolcraft [1856:77 or M. L. Williams 1956:230].

Aitkin and the Ojibwa

Jacques LePique

A young man named Aitkin was running a trading post for his father at Lac de Poteau.[101] Late in the fall, a young Ojibwa came to buy his provisions for the winter, as he used to do every year, but Aitkin would not deal with him.

The Ojibwa said: "What is the reason for this? Haven't I always paid what you asked?"

"Yes," said Aitkin. "You have."

"Then why won't you sell me the supplies?"

"Because I don't choose to."

"Very well," said the Indian.

He went away and the next day he came back with some friends, who asked Aitkin what he had against the young Ojibwa, saying that he was a good man and a regular customer. "Does he owe you anything?" asked one. "Is that the reason why you don't want to deal with him?"

"No," answered Aitkin. "He doesn't owe me a cent. All the same, I'm not going to sell him a pound of provisions. And that settles it."

"No, it doesn't," said the Ojibwa. "I ask you again if you will sell me my winter's supplies."

"No," answered Aitkin. "I'll only deal with those I want to, and I won't deal with you."

"All right," said the Indian. He went home, loaded his gun, and returned with it in his hand. The trader was standing at the door of his cabin.

"Look here, Aitkin," said the Ojibwa. "I want to know for the last time. Are you going to let me have the stores?"

"No."

---

[101] Lac de Poteau (Post Lake). In reality young [Alfred] Aitken was killed at Red Cedar, now Cass Lake. No doubt the error was made by Jacques or his informants.

131

"Then," said the Indian, "you shall not have them, either."

He raised his gun and shot the man through the heart. Then he went home to his mother, a widow, and told her what he had done.

"Oh, my son," she said, crying, "They will come and hang you."

"No they won't, Mother," answered the young man, "There isn't rope enough in America. They'll have to go to the old country if they want to get enough rope to hang me."

"You don't know these white men," said the mother. "When they set out to do a thing, they never give up till it is done."

Word of the killing was sent to Aitkin's father at Fond du Lac[102] and he came down with armed men to arrest the Indian. They went to the widow's lodge, and demanded her son. The young Ojibwa came out, saying that if he had done wrong, he deserved to be punished, and would go with them wherever they wished. So they handcuffed him and started for Prairie du Chien, by way of Fond du Lac.

As they traveled along, the young man seemed quite cheerful. At night, in camp, he would sometimes lie on his back, smiling and singing in a low tone, and once the men heard him chuckling.

"What's that you're laughing at?" one of them asked.

"Oh, they are having great times at home," he answered. "The young men and the girls are dancing, and I can't help laughing at their actions."

Every morning he was found without his handcuffs. He would search under the blankets and toss them to old man Aitkin, saying he'd better take them along for he might need them that day.

On the fifth evening from Lac de Poteau he suddenly started up and said: "My friends, I'm sorry to leave you, but I forgot something I wanted to say to my mother."

With that he vanished, and the men saw a bird fly out of camp in the direction from which they had come.

Next morning they started on his trail as soon as it began to get light. He must have taken some very different shapes for at times they saw in the snow the tracks of a great beast with paws ten feet long, then the tracks of a little animal like a field mouse or a mole that sometimes went beneath the crust, and again the marks of vast flapping wings.

"He must have terrible power," said one Frenchman. "It makes no difference," said old Aitkin. "I'll have him yet. I will go to his wigwam and take him again."

"I will go with you," said the Frenchman, "but I will not lay hands on him. He's a terrible man."

---

[102] [Duluth, Minnesota].

Aitkin and the Ojibwa

In the meantime the young Ojibwa had reached home. He said to his mother, "I told you the white man had not rope enough to hang me. They will come again to get me, I see them starting. But I came home, mother, to tell you that so long as this fox's tail hangs here where I put it, you may know that I am safe. But if it falls to the ground you can make up your mind that you will never see me again.

When Aitkin and his men arrived, the young Ojibwa was as ready to go as before and said it was a pity to have brought them back five days' march. This time the party went through to Prairie du Chien. The Governor, having heard the case, was so angry with old Aitkin that he said he had half a mind to hang him.

"Don't you know," said he, "that your son was in the wrong? He had no business to refuse to sell this man his winter supplies. If I had been the Indian, I would have shot him, too. Let the young man go."[103]

---

[103] Some time after taking down this story, I found a contemporary account of the episode in Warren's *History of the Ojibway Nation* [1852:483–484], and from Fonda's "Reminiscences of Wisconsin." These extracts doubtless present, in the main, the real facts. The most striking difference in the Indian version is, of course, the introduction of the supernatural. I suppose that many fabulous stories were originally based, like this, on actual incidents; but it is not often that we can observe the genesis. A comparison of the Ojibwa version with the contemporary written account shows the birth of a popular tale and its development in the course of a generation or two. It is, in a way, a study of myth making.

Editor's Note: According to contemporary reports, Alfred Aitkin was killed between December and January, 1836–1837, because Aitkin had persuaded the Indian's wife to desert her husband. Although acquitted following prolonged deliberations by the jury, the prisoner was said to be the only sober man in the courtroom. (See Fonda *Wisconsin Historical Collections,* Vol. 5, 271).

The Story of a Half-breed

Jacques LePique

In the Canadian Northwest, there was a half-breed boy named Rob, the son of an Indian girl and a Scotch factor of the Hudson's Bay Company. He was reared by his father—grew up a fine, strong lad, well liked at the post, and came to be one of the best hunters in that country.

While riding alone this boy was captured by a band of hostile Weyot, a savage tribe who lived near the Columbia River. They carried him several days' ride to the village of their chief, meaning to torture him; but the old chief, who had no children, took a strong liking for him and adopted him.

So it was that Rob became a member of the tribe living with the old chief as his son. He took quickly to the ways of the Weyot, learning pretty soon to speak their language and to use their weapons. He soon made a name amongst the young men by his hunting and riding.

One day in a prairie to the south on the borders of the Chinook country, Rob got off his horse by a spring at the edge of some timber. At the same time he heard a sound of hoofs, and looking around saw a girl on a fine black horse riding towards him from beyond the timber. Her hair fell free over her shoulders. She was dressed in white buckskin, in the style of the Chinooks. She was so beautiful that Rob stood watching her as she came near. All at once, she jerked back her arm and threw a tomahawk with such good aim that he had to jump aside to avoid it. But what did Rob then do but fetch the tomahawk and give it back to her, standing by her horse, looking her in the eye. The girl raised her tomahawk again, but his eye did not move, and try as she could, she could not strike. She tried three times. Then she got off her horse and handed him the tomahawk. Rob put it in his belt and led the girl's horse to the spring. There he sat down with her and they talked by signs, for they could not understand each others speech. After a while the girl jumped up, and leaped on her horse; but before she rode away, they agreed by signs to meet there again, fixing the day by pointing to the sun.

When Rob got home, his foster-mother asked him what made him look so happy. Then he told the old people how he had met the beautiful Chinook girl and was going to meet her again; and he asked them if they knew her name.

The chief said, "I have never seen this girl, my son, but I know who she is from what you tell us. She is called the Beauty of the Prairie, the daughter of a chief. Every Weyot has heard of her, and you are lucky to please so fine a girl. But take good care; there are young men amongst her own people who would make it bad for you if they knew of this."

Rob met the Beauty of the Prairie on the day agreed and several times again. He began to learn her language, so that they were able to talk a little. But in these meetings he did not forget what the old chief had said and was always pretty wide awake. One day when his sweetheart had left him at the spring he heard something move in the thicket and from the tail of his eye caught sight of a young man sneaking towards him with a bow in his hand. Rob had his bow, too, but pretended not to see his enemy. Then whipping out an arrow he swung round and the two men shot at the same time. Rob was not hit but the young Chinook went down and Rob found that he had killed him.

He did not know what to do. He left the body and went home so downhearted that the old squaw wanted to know what had happened.

"Didn't you see your Beauty of the Prairie today?" She asked.

"Oh yes," said Rob, "I saw her."

"Well, is she faithful to you then?"

"Oh yes, I know she's not unfaithful."

"But there is something wrong," said she. "Come tell us what it is that makes you look so sad."

"Yes, yes," said the old chief, "tell us, my son. For if you are in trouble we must help you; but we can do nothing if you do not tell us."

So then Rob told them.

"Now, my son," said the chief, "this is very bad. You have killed a man of the other tribe, and if they find it out, his people will have to be revenged. There may be trouble. But you are our son and we will stand by you. Do nothing now; just stay home. Perhaps they cannot find out who killed their brave."

But a medicine man of the Chinooks soon told them who it was, and messengers came to the old chief to demand his son. The chief replied that his people would offer presents to the relations of the slain man.

The messengers went back and in a few days a band of Chinooks arrived for a powwow with the Weyot. The two parties were drawn up opposite each other in full war paint; but the Chinooks had their faces blackened in mourning for the man that had been killed. On the ground between, lay a heap of presents gathered among the Weyot. The orator of the Weyot stood out and offered the peace pipe, saying that he hoped the Chinooks would accept the presents and avoid blood.

"For though you can kill the young man," said he, "you will be sorry afterwards, for we will fight you."

The Chinooks took the pipe and all smoked it except the youngest relation of the dead man. He refused it, having most likely been told to do so. The pipe was offered and passed three times, and each time the young boy refused it. Then the orator of the Weyot filled the pipe for the fourth time. He lighted it and said: "We offer you the peace pipe once more. If you refuse it, it will be worse for you, for there will be war. We will not let you harm the son of our chief. But we hope that you will be our friends. So, now, again, I offer you this pipe." It was passed again and this time it was smoked by all. At that both sides set up a shout and clapped their hands. The old chief of the Weyot arose and made a speech. He said that he thanked the Chinooks and said that he was happy that there would be peace.

The Chinooks took their presents and went home. Soon afterwards a messenger came with a present for Rob of seven braves' plumes and seven pairs of moccasins. The old chief told him that the Chinooks had thus acknowledged him as a big brave and that the moccasins meant that they were going to offer him seven wives, and so make him their son-in-law.

The chief said: "They will bring their best women for you to choose from. And you must take the women, too; for if you did not, it would be the same as saying you are not as big a hunter and fighter as they take you for."

So the Chinooks came with their girls. Rob picked out seven of the handsomest, and the first he chose was the Beauty of the Prairie. The women set up their lodges of white buckskin in the village and Rob hunted for them and provided for them, but he loved only the Beauty of the Prairie. The others grew jealous of her, and one by one they left him and went back to their own people. So Rob lived with Beauty of the Prairie alone and they were very happy.

One day Rob fell in with a party of white men who were hunting to the northeast of the Weyot country, and among these was one of his old friends from the trading post.

"Well, well, well!" said he. "Can this be Rob? Where have you been? We've thought you were dead for two or three years."

The Story of a Half-breed

They met several times and the white man was always at him to go back to his father. Rob had told him he was married to an Indian girl and would never leave her, but as the man kept at him, he said at last he would just go to see his father and come right back. His wife would think he was off on a long hunting trip and would not be uneasy. So away he went.

But when Rob got to the post, his father tried to make him stay, and seeing he was bound to go back to the Indians, made him tipsy and would not let him out of the fort. Soldiers were starting for lower Canada and his father sent him away with them to Toronto, to go to college, hoping that there he would forget the Indian girl. But Rob could think of nothing but getting back to her. About the only way to reach the far Northwest in those days was to go with traders of the Hudson's Bay Company, and they had been ordered not to take him. He knew that his wife would believe that he had deserted her. He grew despondent. He would cry for her till his eyes were red—he began to drink, became a drunkard, and died in the streets.

Major Rains

Kawbawgam

This Major Rains was an officer with the British troops sent to America in 1812 to fight in alliance with the Indians against the Yankees. After the war, he returned from Mackinaw to his home in England but later went to Toronto and married. There his wife had a sister. The Major took these two women up to a piece of land he owned about fifty miles below the Sault.

After a while the people saw that Major Rains was living with the other woman, too. It was known that he had six children in England. By these two sisters he had thirty children. He lived there till he died about thirty years ago. There is a town, on the Canadian shore, called Sailors' Encampment, which is supposed to be almost entirely populated by the children of Major Rains. There are about two hundred and fifty of them.

Rains was a most accommodating man. He would do anything for a man but carry him around in his arms.

Jacques LePique's Reminiscences, Preliminary Note

(Homer H. Kidder)

His real name was Francis Nolin but I never heard him called anything but Jacques LePique[104] (Jack of Spades), a nickname given him by the Canadian French, in allusion, I suppose, to his droll manner.

His grandfather, Louis Nolin[105]—in his day a well known and respected, character at the Sault—was of Irish parentage. Left an Orphan in France, in infancy, he was adopted by a French couple, and inheriting some property from them, emigrated to Canada where he settled at the Sault, marrying an Ojibwa girl and later became an Indian trader. Jacques' father, Louis Nolin, the younger, and his mother, Mary, were both Ojibwa half-breeds, born at the Sault.

Jacques' father, like his grandfather, was a trader and apparently a man of some enterprise. He emigrated with his wife to the then remote Red River country, among the uncivilized Crees, and thence to the black hills where Jacques was born, at Blackstone Falls,[106] probably not later than 1820. When violent fighting broke out between the Crees and the Sioux, the family returned to the Red River and lived at Pembanon till Jacques was thirteen years old. Then Indian fighting drove them from Pembanon. With other refugees, they wintered at Fond du Lac on Lake Superior, now Duluth, and the next spring, when Jacques was fourteen, traveled along the south shore of the lake to the old home of the family

---

[104] At least by the whites, Canadians and Americans. The latter commonly called him Jacques le Pete. I do not know what he was usually called in Ojibwa, possibly Buk-kau-kau-duz (a thin fellow) a nickname he had since boyhood. Kawbawgam often called him Jacques or Jack.

[105] See characteristic anecdotes about this Louis Nolin (the elder) in H. R. Schoolcraft [1848:192–194].

[106] "A place," says Jacques, "where there was a black rock in the middle of the stream. I think it is in Montana."

at Sault Ste. Marie. They subsequently moved to other places along the south shore of Lake Superior; and Jacques himself was at times more or less a wanderer. He journeyed far from his native section—to the arctic and the gulf of Mexico and eastward to the seaboard, visiting many of the large cities; but what is more to the point, at one time or another he became familiar with almost every part of the south shore, often traveling about in it, especially by boat and canoe along the lake.

All this comes out interestingly in the very diversified character of the tales that Jacques contributed to this collection. They include old myths—for he was steeped in Ojibwa lore—but in contrast to the more uniformly primitive character of the tales related by Kawbawgam, who talked no language but his own[107] and lived all his days in [one] limited area, Jacques' stories also include many which represent the wandering life of the half breed, the trader and the voyageur—a life very characteristic of the picturesque changes that have passed over Lake Superior in the last century.

---

[107] Jacques spoke Ojibwa, Cree, Canadian French, and fluent English.

Reminiscences of Jacques LePique— A Journey to the Arctic

Jacques LePique

When Jacques LePique was about twelve years old, living with his parents in the Red River Valley, his father took him on a trading expedition to the Artic to get furs and walrus tusks for trade with the Hudson's Bay Company. A party of sixteen left the Red River on horseback about the breakup of winter and traveled northward with a guide across the Cree Country. When they reached the borders of the next tribe, whose name Jacques has forgotten, they left their horses, and taking dog trains, for it was snowing, went on with an interpreter. After crossing the country of that tribe, they took another interpreter, and so on through four tribes in all.

It was now April or May and about as cold as January on Red River. When they got within a hundred miles of the sea, it was always daylight, and the guide said there would be no more woods.

At last they came to the coast and found Eskimo—about a dozen snow huts. There they saw the northern lights,[108] which looked like fire, shining constantly, not shifting as on Lake Superior. They also saw immense icebergs. These Eskimo hunt in canoes made of hide. In hunting walrus, they have spears with thongs attached and bladders to make them float. When the walrus comes up, he is dead. Jacques did not see them hunt but he saw their rig. They had seal hides, too, and some reindeer, but not so many reindeer as tribes further south.

The traders had brought thimbles, knives, trinkets, earrings, ribbons, braids, etc., and in exchange they got furs and walrus tusks. These they packed on dog trains and started back, picking up interpreters and finally their horses, on the way; and they reached the Red River late in autumn, at snow fall.

---

[108] Aurora borealis. It must have been "snow shine" in the sky, as aurora cannot be seen in the daylight.

Adventures on the Prairie
(about 1833)
A Massacre by the Sioux

Jacques LePique

In those days, among the Crees, the young people—boys and girls—used to make hunting trips on the prairie. A party of this kind, numbering about fifty, started on horseback from Pembanon the year after Jacques returned from the Arctic. He was then thirteen, and a girl about twenty, who had taken a great fancy to him, persuaded his parents to let him go with her. Jacques' older brother, Louis, got the horses ready for them—fast runners—and also furnished them with [dried and] pounded meat. Louis himself did not go.

The party, all decked out, paraded by couples several times around the village—then veered off and rode away at a gallop. Some miles out, the prairie opened wide before them. Once in a while they would jump a brook and they passed clumps of trees.

The party traveled towards a place where they hoped to find good hunting. On the fourth day, in the afternoon, they approached a hill. Jacques and the girl he was riding with had fallen behind and the others had got over the brow of the hill when they reached the fort. Urging their horses up the slope to overtake the rest, they suddenly heard a great firing of guns.

The girl said: "There is fighting. Let us hurry on to do our share."

When they got to the top of the hill, they saw a band of Sioux circling about the fort. Their companions were all killed. The Sioux caught sight of them and gave chase. Jacques had a sword and the girl a gun. But they did not have to use their arms; their horses were so fast that they distanced the Sioux.

By sunset they were out of danger but they rode on all night and camped for rest next day in some timber. Then they rode on the next night and reached home. When they reported the massacre a great war party was formed and set out. They went to the scene of the fight, got track of the Sioux, surprised them in their camp over night and killed most of them. Afterwards they returned to bury their dead brothers and sisters.

It was after this fighting began between the Crees and the Sioux that Jacques' family left Pembanon, to escape the danger and trouble, and went down to Lake Superior, where they spent the following winter on their way to the Sault Ste. Marie, the birth place of their parents.

At Fond du Lac, Jacques' father bought a large canoe for their trip along Lake Superior to the Sault. It was a long hard trip, especially for the children, but they came through without sickness or any great trouble.

One day as they passed Presque Isle,[109] they saw a wigwam at the mouth of the Dead River, and going ashore, they found Matji-gijig[110] sitting on a log on the beach, smoking his long pipe and painted up as if for some ceremony.

"Well," said Jacques' father, "what are you doing today?"

"Oh," replied Matji-gijig, "I am doing nothing today, for it is Sunday."

"How do you know it is Sunday?"

"Why, look around," said Matji-gijig. "See how clear and bright it is. There's not a cloud in the sky. So it must be Sunday."

---

[109] Presque Isle at Marquette, Michigan.

[110] Later Jacque LePique's and Kawbawgam's father-in-law.

Jacques' Life at the Sault and on Lake Superior

Jacques LePique

When the family arrived at the Sault they found that Jacques' grandfather, Louis Nolin, had gone to the Red River and must therefore have passed them somewhere on the south shore. But Jacques' maternal uncle, Michael Adolph, a half-breed, gave them a kind reception. His house was about a mile below the rapids on the Canadian side. His daughter, Sophie Adolph, Jacques' cousin, a girl about eighteen years old, was standing there with her sister near a bench, on which Jacques' mother sat down with her boys. Jacques then had two brothers and two sisters. Another brother, Moses, was born a few years later at Grand Island.[111]

The old people were eating and drinking and uncle Michael said: "Why don't you give the young folks something to eat?"

Sophie then gave them something from the table that to Jacques looked like fungus. It was bread, the first he had ever eaten—and he thought it pretty dry. He had been used to fish, eggs, fowl, buffalo meat and other meats. But this was a new kind of life. It was at this time [that] he first tasted an apple and it was at the Sault that he first heard English spoken. About [this] time also he first saw Kawbawgam.

The family spent the first winter at Michael Adolph's and the next winter they stayed on the American side. Then American Fur Company engaged Jacques' father to run a trading post at Bay Furnace and Grand Island. The following spring they went to the Sault with furs, and again the spring after that, when he first saw Charlotte, afterwards Kawbawgam's wife, then a baby on a cradle board. Her father was Matji-gijig, a chief, whom Jacques had seen at the mouth of Dead River, on the trip from the head of the lake to the Sault.

---

[111] Louis and Mary Nolin's children, in the order of birth, were Louis, Louisa, Jacques or Francis, Angeline, Joseph, and Moses.

Life at the Sault and on Lake Superior

A half-breed named Dube from Saginaw, president of a company whose name Jacques does not recall, persuaded Louis Nolin to leave the American Fur Company and keep his own post at Grand Island. The Nolins stayed there two years more. Moses was born at Bay Furnace in April the last spring that Louis Nolin was with the American Fur Company.

The next winter they went back to the Sault and after that lived about from place to place for several years. It was during this time that they heard that Queen Victoria was crowned; and that year Jacques' mother died (1837).

Later on Jacques shipped before the mast on the topsail schooner *Florence* on Lake Superior. In the fall, the Schooner *Caroline* came up to the Sault, and Jacques shipped in her for the round trip to Detroit and back.

Still later, a propeller, the *Independence,* was hauled up over the rapids and sailed on Lake Superior; Jacques was on her all the following summer (1844) before the mast. About September, Jacques and some other young fellows agreed to go down to Lake Huron, in the country around Alpena and Thunder Bay, to hunt and trap. There they spent the winter and in the spring of 1845 they went down to Detroit to sell their furs. In Detroit, Jacques fell in with his father and by him was introduced to Col. Berry, Mr. S. T. Carr and Mr. Philo Everett. They were standing on Jefferson Avenue. These gentlemen had the summer before been up to Iron Bay and what later became Marquette Harbor.

It was these men from Jackson, Michigan, who opened the iron mining industry on Lake Superior. Jacques' father, who spoke broken English, had been with the party as interpreter, for Matji-gijig [their guide] understood no English.

Jacques then went back to Thunder Bay and thence to the Sault where he again met the Jackson Mine party, among whom, besides some of those he had met at Detroit, were Fairchild, Monroe and Kirklaws. Jacques joined the party, on board the *Independence,* which landed them at the mouth of Dead River. They took a canoe around the shore to Lighthouse Point after passing Kawbawgam's camp about where Prior's boathouse now stands.[112] Kawbawgam and three or four other Ojibwas were engaged by the party—the *Independence* having gone back—and they all went around into Iron Bay to cut a road. An old squaw was cook. They began the road where the Rolling Mill Store is and Kawbawgam cut the first tree.[113] Jacques, not being much of an axe man, was detailed as

---

[112] I think Prior's boathouse was at the foot of Hewitt Avenue.

[113] This, in its way, was an event in local history. The cutting of the first tree in opening a road to the mines was the beginning of the town of Marquette as port of shipment for the ore.

packer to carry pork over from Dead River. He stayed two or three months and then returned to the Sault in a bark canoe with a half-breed named John Roussau (a brother of Kawbawgam's sister)[114] and Congress Ord, son of the Indian agent at the Sault. Jacques then went back on the *Independence,* this time as a stoker and later became an under engineer or oiler.

[In the] meantime Jacques' father had died and he had the care of his sisters and youngest brother. He wanted to go to the Red River to look up some relations. On the way, he saw the *Michigan* lying at LaPointe. On board was a half-breed lawyer and mason named John Martel, well known to Jacques. This man told him that an Ojibwa mission was about to start for Washington with the object of recovering from the government certain lands about Lac de Flambeau which the Indians of that neighborhood wanted as a reservation; and he persuaded Jacques to go along as an interpreter. Jacques signed a paper, received money for traveling expenses, and setting out from LaPointe with this Martel and two Indians, joined the mission at the Brulé River, on the way to St. Paul, where they were to take a steamboat down the Mississippi. The mission included four chiefs,[115] of whom one was a war chief and another an orator. These chiefs held a council on the Brulé and several other Ojibwas decided to go with the delegation. In all, fourteen people started, not counting the canoe men hired to take them as far as Stillwater. Before they reached St. Croix, they became uneasy about the Sioux. The chief from Lac Vieux Desert was a medicine man and they gave him some tobacco. He rattled the deer-hoofs and said he saw no danger from the Sioux but said that on the journey to Washington someone was going to die.

"When we get to Washington," said he, "the President is going to give us five boxes of money."[116] "But," said the medicine man, "you had

---

Editor's Note: According to an 1884 map of Marquette, located at the Marquette County Historical Society, the Rolling Mill was located near the present-day Shiras Steam Plant on Lake Street, at the base of the bluff.

[114] I suppose this must mean a half-brother of Kawbawgam's half-sister. Kawbawgam's mother was apparently married several times. The ease with which marriage was terminated with one person and contracted with another resulted in some complicated relationships among the offspring.

[115] These were: A war chief from Lac de Flambeau named E-ni-wa-bun-ung (Overlooking the Whole Country); a chief from Fond du Lac (orator of the mission) named Nin-gaw-nub (Sitting at the Front); a chief named Shi-baw-gi-zhik (Hole in the Day); and a chief, not named, from Lac Vieux Desert. Besides Nin-gaw-nub's wife and child there was another young woman; and there were two braves, not chiefs, named Gish-calk (Cut Tree) from Fond du Lac, and Wa-gi-wi-ne (Crooked Horn) from Leach Lake—all these were original members of the mission. The others joined after the council, at the Brulé.

[116] Meaning five thousand dollars.

better watch anyway, for if the Sioux over on the mainland[117] have a medicine man, his power may offset mine, and so I may not be able to see some danger that is perhaps awaiting us. To test the truth of what I am telling you, you can look for rain tomorrow afternoon. And we shall see an animal on the left bank going down. This animal is sent to us by the Great Spirit. We shall kill it. Soon after that we shall meet a canoe with two Indians and a white man in the center. If you see all that, you can know that what I tell you tonight is going to happen."

The party reached the Mississippi a little before the freeze up and took a steamer down to St. Louis. John Martel got up an Indian show. They rented Corinthian Hall and made some money giving their dances. Then they took another boat, the *Mondiana,* to Cairo, and another, the *Swallow,* to New Orleans. Having exhibited there for two weeks, in Nymphs' Hall, they returned in the *Arrow* to Cairo and thence went up the Ohio River in the steamer *Kentucky* to Louisville, where they gave another show.

"By that time money was running low. The *Kentucky* fetched us to Cincinnati, [we] exhibited there and made enough money to get to Pittsburgh. John Martel ran the business. We went from Cincinnati by stage to Franklin, Columbus, Zanesville and Wheeling and from Wheeling took another boat to Pittsburgh."

At Pittsburgh, Martel made the acquaintance of a fellow Mason, Captain May, who paid the fare of the party to Philadelphia. The young chief Hole-in-the-Day, however, was taken sick and Jacques stayed with him while he was in the hospital. After three weeks, Jacques told Captain May that the chief was now getting better and could stand the trip so they spent two days with May before taking the stage across the Allegheny Mountains to Harrisburg. There they got a train. A man named Snodgrass asked them if they had any money. Jacques said, "Yes, $3.00 borrowed from Captain May." Without being asked, Snodgrass gave them $15.00. The train got snowed in and it took five engines to pull it out.

"[We] got to Philadelphia and found our party again. They were staying in the Red Lion Hotel on Market Street, at the corner of South Street. A circus (had) hired our people to exhibit. But it was now about time to be getting to Washington."

After another week in Baltimore at the Exchange Hotel, the mission at last reached the Capital, arriving in the night and went to the Steamboat Hotel, Pennsylvania Avenue, run by a man named West.

Polk was President. Taylor was in Mexico. Martel arranged an interview with the President and also with the Commissioner of Indian

---

[117] They were camped on an island in the St. Croix River.

Affairs, Colonel Madill or Madeo. They went first to Madill. He did not understand the Indians' demands and said he could not supply them with funds to travel back, but would give them a good word to the President. An officer was taking them round. They said goodbye to Colonel Madill and were driven to the White House. They saw a little man in a stove pipe hat; this was President Polk. Jacques had expected to see a man with crown and scepter.

The Indians sat down in a room. The President greeted them and after offering them cigars and whiskey asked the trouble. John then explained they wanted some lands around Lac de Flambeau as a reservation. The President said that this would have to go before Congress and also the matter of getting funds to travel home, for which he advised them to get up a petition with signatures of prominent men. Ebenezer Warner drew up the petition. Some members of the House wanted the Indian orator to give them a talk about Indian affairs and life and to tell them how the Indians were being treated. So before the petition was presented, Nigawnub gave a talk in the House and Jacques interpreted. The petition went in the next day and Congress voted them $5,000 to go back. But they did not get their reservation. In fact, this matter did not go before Congress.

A week later, the President entertained the whole party at supper. He and his wife, at the head of the table, were the only persons present not in Indian costume. The plates and glasses were turned upside down. Under the glasses were papers and under each plate was $40.00 in gold and a gold ring. The papers were orders on a military store for a suit of clothes.

"My red children," said Polk, "the presents under the plates are from your Great Mother (his wife); the presents under the glasses are from me."

Music started up and all was so fine that Martel said he could not eat and asked Jacques if it did not remind him of the Arabian Nights. Jacques couldn't eat either. When supper was over the table was cleared and they gave the President a war dance. Afterwards they drew their money and went west. The party traveled to Chicago and up the Mississippi to St. Paul, from there to their homes in the Minnesota Lake Country. But [Jacques] went to Detroit and so to the Sault.

After that, he returned to Washington every winter for four years as [a] hired interpreter. But when it became known that the interpreters were to be discharged, one of them suggested resigning. They all did so. John Martel drew up the resignation.

Coming in the spring from Washington, Jacques was married in the fall to Kawbawgam's younger sister, Mary, then about thirteen years old.

The next year, having moved to L'Anse, they lost their house and belongings by fire. They crossed over by snowshoe to Kawbawgam's little house on the hill above the Marquette Rolling Mill, and the next year built a house at Presque Isle. In one year it was burned. In a year or two he built another house there, and in all he lived at Presque Isle for ten years. They afterwards moved to Chocolay [River].

Once when Jacques was going by train to Negaunee to sing with Mary in a choir, a cinder flew into his eye and he was nearly blind for ten years. During this time they lived in the Carp House, a house[118] that Mr. Hiram Burt had built for the new employees in the Rolling Mill, and when the mill was abandoned, Mr. Burt put Jacques and Mary into the house as caretakers. Afterwards they lived in winter at Light House [Point] and in summer at the German Settlement [Green Garden near the upper Chocolay River], where he afterwards bought forty acres and built a house near Kawbawgam's.

Ed Sawonon's squaw began to suffer from fits. In one of these, Colonel Kidder[119] brought her to, by putting his hands on her head. In talking it over, she said she needed a medicine man. So they sent to L'Anse for a medicine man named Bush-quay-gin (Leather). He came down by train and built a medicine lodge at the German Settlement. It was like a round screen, shaped like a barrel[120] about eight feet high and open at the top, having six poles and six hoops. It was two fathoms around, that is about four feet in diameter and the poles were covered round with a sail. Bush-quay-gin wanted scarlet cloth to cover the frame but could not get it.

When the medicine lodge was finished it was getting towards twilight. These performances should begin just at dusk in the evening. Jacques' wife was leading him for he couldn't see very well after dark. He and Mary sat down near the medicine lodge.

Jacques heard a voice above say: "We can do nothing for this woman. She is not pure."

Once in a while they heard the song of a robin, wash-ka-ka-ka-ka.

"But the man," said the voice, "sitting there holding his wife's hand, we can help him."

So Mary led him up and spread a blanket beside the lodge. Jacques lay down on it and put his head into the lodge, under a little flap next to the ground. His head lay close to the medicine man who sat inside. For

---

[118] Run by Jason Mc Gregor's father [see note 126].

[119] Winslow Kidder, a cousin of my father. He was an army engineer and built the Marquette breakwater for the U.S. government. *Editor's Note:* Ed Sawonon may be a version of *Shawonong* Kawbawgam's brother (see note 60).

[120] JEA Cylinder.

a good while there was no sound. Then he heard a voice above saying: "Now is the time to go and blow on him." Another voice answered: "Then why don't you blow on him?" With that Jacques heard a noise like that of claws coming down the pole next to his head. He then felt a cold wind blowing on his head, it seemed as if his eyes would freeze. The water ran from them and he felt as if they were being pulled out. Then the noise of scratching claws went back up the pole.

As the spirit went up, a voice above asked: "What did you do for him?"

The spirit answered: "This man once got a piece of iron in his eye but now I have taken it out. He will see very well all day tomorrow."

The other spirit said: "I wouldn't thank anyone to give me my sight for one day."

"Well," said the first, "that's all I can do for him. If you can do so much more, you'd better go down and try."

Jacques heard the other coming down and felt the same cold wind. When this spirit went back up the pole, the first one said: "What did you do for him? You don't seem to have anything in your bill?"

They sounded like birds talking. What they said was interpreted by another spirit that was invisible except for a light like sulphur which went out when he ceased speaking. His voice was no bigger than a baby's. In interpreting, he addressed each spirit as his grandfather.

"Well," said the second, "I have done enough so that this man's sight will get better from this time forth, to the end of his life."

Jacques then got up, and accordingly his sight steadily improved till he could see perfectly. At present (1895) he has remarkably good vision. As he told me this, he pointed to a vessel lying about a quarter of a mile off and said: "I can see every rope and halyard on that schooner." His hearing, as I have found in hunting deer with him, is more acute than mine.

After building his house at the German Settlement and helping Kawbawgam to build there, too, Jacques took part in building a club house for Mr. Ripca. There he used to see Mr. Huey Fay and Mr. Walton Duane, who was called Bay-be-wah-kun-see-gah-dayd (Slim Legs). My father, Alfred Kidder, they called Te-quah-bit (Glass Eyes). They called me Te-quah-bince (Little Glass Eyes).

Jacques first met my father in the spring of 1863 and went exploring with him on the head waters of the Salmon Trout and Yellow Dog, going inland from Big Bay. The mosquitoes were terrible. He was in the woods with my father off and on all that summer and winter and in 1864.

This ends Jacques' narrative. His wife, Mary, was drowned at the northwest point of Presque Isle.[121] Afterwards he lived for some years in a little cabin he had on the upper bayou of Whitefish Lake where I went two or three times to stay with him (1893–95) hunting and taking down some of these tales. (The rest of the tales were taken down at Kawbawgam's house on Presque Isle).

When Jacques got too old to do for himself he was pensioned by Peter White, Samuel P. Ely, J. M. Longyear and my father, who had all known and liked him for many years. He spent his last days in Red River Valley, in Manitoba, Canada, "tenderly cared for" my father was told, by the family with whom he lived for years. There Jacques LePique died of old age.

---

[121] *Editor's Note:* From H. H. Kidder's letter to Mrs. Carroll Paul published in *The Mining Journal,* March 12, 1937: "Jacques and Mary after provisioning at Marquette for a trip up the lake—imbibing rather too copiously as Indians were likely to do when 'treating' among friends at the moment of taking leave—started off in a bark canoe. They may have struck choppy seas on rounding Presque Isle or it may be that they were, by that time, too drunk to sit up. Anyway the canoe capsized in the shallow water that lies on those shelving rocks at the northwest point. Jacques scrambled ashore and not till then, though I don't know how soon, noticed that Mary wasn't with him. This seems to have brought him to his senses. He saw her in the water and dragged her out, drowned. He told me it pretty nearly killed him when he found she was dead. He didn't tell me that he had been drinking—that I learned from my father, who was evidently informed of the circumstances, though I think all this happened a good while before he went to Lake Superior in 1861. Jacques was no drunkard and I have understood was devoted to Mary. She seems to have been a good woman, a good wife to Jacques."

Overland Trails

Kawbawgam and Jacques LePique

When asked to tell me of some of the old overland trails in the Lake Superior country (south side) Kawbawgam said: There was a trail from Grand Island, Kitchi minising, on Lake Superior, to Little Bay de Noc, weequay dousing[122] (small bay) on Lake Michigan; and another trail from Grand Island, to Au Train, Madawbawnighk [123] (the end of the trail on the beach) or, (where the trail comes down on the beach.) There was a trail from Old Masonville, on the Escanaba River, Aush kon aw bay sibi[124] (the young man river) to the mouth of the Chocolay on Lake Superior.[125] Connecting with this trail another ran from Iron Bay, Lake Superior, over to L'Anse, Lake Superior. It started in about where the Rolling Mill is,[126] ran first to Teal Lake, Shingebiss ah go mud (where the hell-diver stays in the water) from there to Lake Michigamme, Michi gau mig (resort of the big spirit)[127] thence to Three Lakes, Ah-yah-yah-nek-kay-goh-mog[128] (the following lakes) and from there to L'Anse, Wee quay dungk [129] (a bay).

From L'Anse, a trail ran through the woods to Lac Vieux Desert,

---

[122] *Editor's Note:* Wiikwedoonsing (in a small bay [locative])—J. D. Nichols.

[123] *Editor's Note:* Madabon ingk.

[124] *Editor's Note:* Oshkinawe sibi.

[125] *Editor's Note:* See "Two Stories of Sauks Head" (p. 116). Local traditions published by C. Fred Rydholm mention a trail along the Carp River to Teal Lake where it split into two parallel trails to Lake Michigamme from which there was canoe access by way of the Michigamme and Menominee Rivers to Lake Michigan (1989:69–70).

[126] *Editor's Note:* According to an 1884 map of Marquette, the Rolling Mill was located near the present-day Shiras Steam Plant on Lake Street at the base of the bluff.

[127] *Editor's Note:* kitchigami (big lake) (Baraga 1878:I, 152).

[128] *Editor's Note:* ayayaanikegamaag (where there is a chain of lakes) J. D. Nichols.

[129] *Editor's Note:* wi-kwedong (Baraga 1878:I, 24)

Kay tay ki ti gau ning[130] (old garden) thence to Lac de Poteau, Kah kah ah gon ing sagah eegun (post lake) thence to the Mississippi River at Prairie du Chien, Kay bay zaw wagay (running dammed or choked). From Lac de Poteau the trail split in three branches, namely: the one just mentioned to Prairie du Chien; another to Stillwater, *kee gauago* mud (where the fish lie in the water); and another to St. Croix, Minominikay shen sibi ka kabikaw[131] (?) (rice river falls).

---

[130] *Editor's Note:* katikitegon (Kinietz 1947)

[131] *Editor's Note:* mánoominikeshiinh (rice bird) J. D. Nichols sibi (river), kakabikawan (cascade).

Some Ojibwa Place Names[132]

Kawbawgam and Jacques LePique

The names are in the order the places occur along the lake, beginning with Point Abbaye on the west:

Point Abbaye (French: *au beignet,* fritter) between L'Anse Bay and Huron
  Bay: Kit-chi né-aw-shing[133]
Huron Islands: O me nah ah ko naw ningk[134]
Huron Bay: Sibi (?) we gaum mi gung[135]
Big Huron River: Kitchi maw ees swa gun Sibi[136]

---

[132] My spelling of these names, as of other Ojibwa words in the texts, is obviously untutored; nor, being ignorant of the language, can I answer for the correctness of the sounds I have tried to record. From this record, such as it is, however, I do not doubt that an Ojibwa scholar could, in most cases, recognize and correct the sounds intended by my informants.
  Editor's Note: The following citations from Kidder present problems not the least of which is misreading Kidder's spellings. His Ojibwa place names are noted together with a recent study by Bernard C. Peters and reference to Frederick Baraga's Ojibwa dictionary. John D. Nichols asserts that in several cases Peters has the name wrong and Kidder has it right. "For example, [Peters] has added an inappropriate prefix ni 'my' to the "head" part of Sauks Head Lake, by using Baraga's citation form for head (Personal Communication, Jan. 8, 1991). Admittedly, some editorial notes are speculative but are offered as a start for those who treasure and identify with the heritage of these landmarks.

[133] *Editor's Note:* According to Bernard C. Peters, (1981:249. kitchi nei ashing (big point place).

[134] *Editor's Note:* omahwungeaun wahkanug ingk (place of the gathering of edible moss [lichen]) [Peters 1981:248].

[135] *Editor's Note:* wikwedong (in a bay), *ung* (place) [Peters 1981:248–249].

[136] *Editor's Note:* kitchi mawandjiss wakon sibi (large gathering [place] of edible moss), sibi (river) [Peters:248].

Some Ojibwa Place Names

Spruce Pine River (Pine River): Kah oh ke kah dah go kog Sibi[137]

Spruce Pine Lake (Pine Lake): Kah oh ke kah dah go kog Sawga-weegun[138]

Conway Lake: We quay daw wah gaw saw qaweegun[139]

Salmon Trout River: Maw shah may go see koog Sibi[140]

Big Bay: Kitchie way quay dung[141]

Lake Independence: Kitchi way quay dung Sawgaweegun[142]

Yellow Dog River: Shaw zha wah gum e nong Sibi[143]

Sauks Head: Ozah gee wush te gwong ah go dayg[144]

Sauks Head Lake: Ozahgee wush te gwong Saw gaw eegun[145]

Sauks Head Island: Ozahgee wush te gwong a go dayg minis (island where the Sauk heads hang)[146]

Garlic River: See gaw ga wush sekong (?) Sibi[147]

Little Presque Isle River: Misquah be kaw Sibi (red rock river)[148]

Little Presque Isle: Misquah be kaw Singk[149]

Little Presque Isle Lake: Misquah be kaw Saw gaweegun[150]

Sugar Loaf Mountain: Do-do-so-ak-i-nong (woman's breast)[151]

Presque Isle: Kah way komigong nay aw shay (point of jealousy)[152]

---

[137] *Editor's Note:* kog sibi (spruce [place] river) [Peters 1981:248].

[138] *Editor's Note:* kog sagaiigan (spruce [place] lake) [Peters 1981:248].

[139] *Editor's Note:* wikwedong (in a bay) wágá sagaiigan (crooked inland lake) [Baraga 1878:I, 24, 153].

[140] *Editor's Note:* majamegoss kong sibi (brook trout [place] river) [Peters 1981:247].

[141] *Editor's Note:* wikwedong (in a bay) [Baraga 1878:I, 24].

[142] *Editor's Note:* wikwedong sagaiigan (large bay lake) [Baraga 1878:I, 24].

[143] shaw zha wah gum e gong: ball with foggy gray color—no natural color? way daw we sid ani mosh: a yellow dog. I do not know that this name was ever applied to the river or place by the Ojibwas, but see the reference to the name in my paper "Two Local Indian Traditions."

   Editor's Note: osawa gume nong sibi (yellow water [place] river) [Peters 1984:247].

[144] *Editor's Note:* osagi nishtigwan ogodeg (where the Sauk heads hang) [Peters 1984:111].

[145] *Editor's Note:* osagi nishtigwan ogodeg sagaiigan (the lake where the Sauk heads hang) [Peters 1984:111].

[146] *Editor's Note:* osagi nishtigwan ogodeg miniss (island where the Sauk heads hang) [Peters 1984:111].

[147] *Editor's Note:* shiggawgawinzheegong sibi (skunkweed or onion river) [Peters 1984:246].

[148] *Editor's Note:* miskwa ajibika sibi (red rock river) [Peters 1984:246].

[149] *Editor's Note:* miskwa ajibika sink (place of the red rock) [Peters 1984:246].

[150] *Editor's Note:* miskwa ajibik sagaiigan (red rock lake) [Peters 1984:246].

[151] *Editor's Note:* totoshinong (place of the woman's breast) [Peters 1984:245].

[152] *Editor's Note:* gáwe win kamigong neiaáshi (jealousy ground [place] point of land) [Peters 1984:245].

Dead River: Kah way komigong nay aw shay Sibi[153]
Light House Point: Pah gee dah ah bay wee nay sing (set a line)[154]
Carp River (near Marquette): Namay binè Sibi[155]
Chippewa Lookout: Ozah gee ah kaw wah bee win (Sauk's watch or
    lookout)[156]
Big Entry: Kitchi Saw ging (I don't know where this is)[157]
Shot Point: Ah nee kay dah wah gong (the next sand beach)[158]
Sand River: Ah neekay dah wah gong Sibi[159]
Laughing White Fish: Odekomag (Adikameg?) sibi[160]
Whitefish River: Ohnemis kawning (place where we kill pigeons)[161]
Sucker Lake: Kish ke quay denung Sawgaw eegun (cut hand mountain
    lake)[162]
Rock River: Zhosh quah naw be kaw Sibi (slippery rock river)[163]
Au Train Island: Mah daw bon Minis[164]
Au Train Lake: Mah daw bon Sawgaweegun[165]
Au Train: Mah daw bon ingk (going down or getting down, but in the list
    of "Overland Trails" it is rendered 'end of trail or beach,' or 'where
    the trail comes down on the beach')[166]
Grand Island: Kitchi Minising[167]
Williams Point (Grand Island): Kay tay o da na (old village)[168]

---

[153] *Editor's Note:* gáwe win kamigong sibi (jealousy ground place river) [Peters 1984:245].

[154] *Editor's Note:* pagidabi winawaing (they set a line with hooks to catch fish place) [Peters 1984:244].

[155] *Editor's Note:* namebin sibi (sucker river) [Peters 1984:244].

[156] *Editor's Note:* osagi okawia inabiwin (Sauk tracking lookout) [Peters 1984:243–244].

[157] *Editor's Note:* kitchi sawging (big river mouth place—Chocolay River) [Peters 1984:243], gitchy seebing (1836 Treaty, Washington).

[158] *Editor's Note:* ani ah nee mitawang ong (there is a little sandy beach) [Peters 1984:243].

[159] *Editor's Note:* ani ah nee mitawanga ong sibi (there is a little sandy beach river) [Peters 1984:243].

[160] *Editor's Note:* atikameg sibi bapwin (whitefish river laughing) [Peters 1984:242–243].

[161] *Editor's Note:* omimi (wild pigeons) [Baraga 1878:I, 193].

[162] *Editor's Note:* kishkinindjiodis (cut off his hand) wadjiw (mountain) sagaiigan (inland lake) [Baraga 1878:I, 125,l74, 153].

[163] *Editor's Note:* joshkwamagad ajibik sibi (slippery rock river) [Peters 1984:242].

[164] *Editor's Note:* madabon miniss (to go on a river in a canoe to the lake island [river of the trail]) [Peters 1984:241].

[165] *Editor's Note:* madabon sagaiigan (to go on a river in a canoe to the lake) [Peters 1984:241].

[166] *Editor's Note:* madabon ingk (place where trail comes down to beach) [Peters 1984:241].

[167] *Editor's Note:* kitchi minissing (place of the great island) [Peters 1984:240–241].

[168] *Editor's Note:* geté (ancient) odéna (village) [Baraga 1878:I, 12,178].

Some Ojibwa Place Names

Powells Point: Shing gwa kosh puduk ee zud (where the little pine tree stands[169]

Annes Bay: Kishe (wa) quay wee dong (cedar)[170]

---

[169] *Editor's Note:* jingwak (young pine tree), patakidé (stands up) [Baraga 1878:I, 193,243].

[170] *Editor's Note:* gijik (cedar tree), wikwedong (in a bay)[Baraga 1878:I, 45, 24].

Ojibwa Names of the Twelve Moons or Months of the Year

Kawbawgam and Jacques LePique

January: Kitchi monedo gizis (moon of the big spirit)[171]
February: Namabini gizis (sucker or carp moon)[172]
March: Ona ba ni gizis (the moon of crust on the snow)[173]
April: Pay po quay dah gim gizis (snow shoe breaking moon)[174]
May: Wah bi gua ni gizis (the moon of flowers)[175]
June: Ou day i men gizis (the moon of strawberries)[176]
July: Mis qui mi ni gizis (the moon of raspberries)[177]
August: Mini gizis once (little huckleberry moon)[178]
September: Kitchi mean gizis (big huckleberry moon)[179]
October: Namagosi gizis (the moon of trout)[180]
November: Adikamémégo gizis (the moon of white fish)[181]
December: Manedo gizis once (little spirit moon)[182]

---

[171] *Editor's Note:* According to Baraga (1878: I, 148), manitogisis.

[172] *Editor's Note:* namebini-gisiss (Baraga 1878I, 98).

[173] *Editor's Note:* onábanad (snow is crusty) [Baraga 1878:I, 236], onabani-gisiss [Baraga 1878:I, 166].

[174] *Editor's Note:* agim (snowshoe) [Baraga 1878:I, 236], bebodwedagiming-gisiss (April) [Baraga 1878:I, 15].

[175] *Editor's Note:* wabigoni (yellow flower), gisiss (May) [Baraga 1878:I, 168].

[176] *Editor's Note:* odéimini-gisiss (June) [Baraga 1878:I, 149].

[177] *Editor's Note:* miskwimini-gisiss (July) [Baraga 1878:I, 149].

[178] *Editor's Note:* min-gisiss (moon of bilberries) [Baraga 1878:II, 241].

[179] *Editor's Note:* manomini-gisiss (September) [Baraga 1878:I, 224].

[180] *Editor's Note:* namégossi (place where there are trout) [Baraga 1878:I, 270], bina kwi-gissis (October) [leaves of trees fall off, Baraga 1878:I, 148, II 85].

[181] *Editor's Note:* atikameg (whitefish) [Baraga 1878:I, 287].

[182] *Editor's Note:* manitogisissons [Baraga 1878:I, 68].

Notes on Kawbawgam

Homer H. Kidder

Charles Kawbawgam, or Nawaquay-geezhik, was born at or near the Sault Ste. Marie, the son of Muk-kud-day-wuk-kwud [Black Cloud], an Ojibwa chief. His earliest recollection is of General Lewis Cass's first visit to the Sault in the year 1820 though Kawbawgam thought it was in 1812.

I am not certain whether I have noted elsewhere that Kawbawgam told me (through Jacques LePique) that he remembered on that day, seeing his uncle walk up the hill, where the Fort now is, wearing a British officer's red coat, which he had received from the English at the time of the earlier treaty. The intention was, I believe, to express the loyalty of the Ojibwas to the British. As this incident was the first thing that Kawbawgam could remember, he must have been a very young boy, probably not over five or six years old, in 1820. It would seem quite improbable that he was over ten, so that at most he could hardly have been over 92 when he died on December 28, 1902. I am inclined to believe he was not much over 87 or 88. He always said he did not know his own age, but for years before he died, he was popularly supposed to be over a hundred years old. Owing to his mistake in getting it fixed in his mind that Cass's visit to the Sault was in 1812, he doubtless supposed himself to be older than he was.

His original name was Nawaquay-geezhik (Noon Day). Kawbawgam was a pet name given by his mother when he was a small boy. I do not know what it means.

Appendix

Order of Narratives and Supplementary Materials in H. H. Kidder's Manuscript, "Ojibwa Myths and Halfbreed Tales"

Introductory Note
Nanabozho (Kawbawgam)
Kawbawgam's Remarks on Nana-
bozho
Nanabozho in Time of Famine (Kaw-
bawgam)
Nanabozho Plays at Being Dead (Kaw-
bawgam)
The Lost War Party (Kawbawgam)
The Beast Men (Jacques LePique)
The Great Skunk (Kawbawgam)
The Great Bear of the West (Kaw-
bawgam)
The Great Skunk and The Great Bear
of the West (Homer H. Kidder)
Wampum Hair (Jacques LePique)
The Girls and the Porcupine (Kaw-
bawgam)
Chickadee Boy (Kawbawgam)
The Girl and the Midéwug (Jacques
LePique)
Paying the Devil (Jacques LePique)
Kwasind (Jacques LePique)
The Man Who Died Three Times
(Jacques LePique)
The Jessakkiwin and the Midé (Kaw-
bawgam)
The Robin (Jacques LePique)
The Whippoorwill (Kawbawgam)

The Sister's Ghost (Charlotte Kaw-
bawgam)
The League of the Four Upper Algon-
quian Nations (Kawbawgam)
Some Ojibwa History (Kawbawgam)
Fight with the Iroquois (Kawbawgam)
Sauks at Portage Entry (Jacques
LePique)
Wyagaw (Kawbawgam)
The Thunder Birds and the Medicine
Root (Kawbawgam)
Mishi Ginabig & the Thunder Birds
(Kawbawgam)
Mishi Ginabig in Lake Michigamme
(Jacques LePique)
Water Spirits in Sable Lake (Jacques
LePique)
The Curing of I-que-wa-gun (Kaw-
bawgam)
The Great Turtle (Kawbawgam)
The Iron Maker (Jacques LePique)
Fragment of a Medicine Story
(Jacques LePique)
Nibawnawbé (Homer H. Kidder)
A Famine and How a Medicine Man
Saved the People (Kawbawgam)
The Cedar Knife (Jacques LePique)
The Midéwiwin (Kawbawgam)
The Jessakkiwin (Kawbawgam)

APPENDIX

Fasting and Medicine Songs (Jacques LePique)

The Snow Rabbit and the North Wind (Homer H. Kidder)

Our Brother-in-Law's Adventures (Kawbawgam)

The Man from the World Above (Jacques LePique)

Aitkin and the Ojibwa (Jacques LePique)

Note on the "Story of a Half-Breed" [no text]

The Story of a Half-Breed (Jacques LePique)

Jacques LePique's Reminiscences Preliminary note (Homer H. Kidder)

Reminiscences of Jacques LePique

A Journey to the Artic

Adventures on the Prairie Jacques LePique's Life at the Sault and on Lake Superior

Ojibwa Names of the Moons (Kawbawgam and Jacques LePique)

Some Ojibwa Names of Places (Kawbawgam and Jacques LePique)

Overland Trails (Kawbawgam and Jacques LePique)

Anecdotes (Kawbawgam and Jacques LePique)

Appendix and Notes

Note on Parentage, etc. (Kawbawgam)

The Diver (Kawbawgam)

Extracts from W. J. Hoffman

Major Rains (Kawbawgam)

Jesuit Relations for Reference

Note on Upper Algonquians

Extracts from Baraga's Dictionary

"Hiawatha and Other Legends"

Extracts from McGuire's Ethnology in the Jesuit Relations

Extracts from Michelson's Notes, etc.

Wm. Jones' Biography

Note on Muskrat by Dr. G. M. Allen

Extract from Warren's History of the Ojibwas

Extract from Fonda's Reminiscences

My Father's Episode from Jacques LePique Legend (Jacques LePique)

Extract from Charlevoix

Concerning Mermen from my diary, etc.

Indians on War Raids, extract from Fonda

"Tales of an Indian Camp," by J. A. Jones

Peabody Museum, Cambridge

From Marquette Mining Journal, "Two Local Traditions."

Bibliography

Allen, James.
1832 Journal (in Philip P. Mason, *Schoolcraft's Expedition to Lake Itasca.* 1958. Lansing, Michigan, 170).
Baraga, Frederic.
1847 *Chippewa Indians.* (Studio Slovenica 10) H. R. Schoolcraft Collection, Library of Congress. New York, Washington, 1976.
1878 *A Dictionary of the Otchipwe Language, Explained in English.* 2 Parts, (Reprinted 1973, Minneapolis).
Barnouw, Victor.
1955 "A Psychological Interpretation of a Chippewa Origin Legend," *Journal of American Folklore,* 68: 73–85, 211–223, 341–355.
1977 *Wisconsin Chippewa Myths & Tales and Their Relation to Chippewa Life.* Madison, Wisconsin.
Blackbird, Andrew J.
1887 *History of the Ottawa and Chippewa Indians of Michigan, and Grammar of Their Language.* Ypsilanti, Michigan.
Bush, Martha.
1988 "Amazing Upper Peninsula Women," *Marquette Monthly* 6 (March): 19–21.
Chamberlain, Alexander F.
1891 "Nanibozhu amongst the Otchipwe, Mississagas, and Other Algonkian Tribes," *Journal of American Folklore* 4: 193–213.
Coleman, M. Bernard, Ellen Frogner, and Estelle Eich.
1961 *Ojibwa Myths and Legends.* Minneapolis.
de Jong, Josselin J. P. B de.
1913 "Original Odzibwe Texts," *Beiträge zur Völkerkunde, Leipzig (Herausgegeben aus Mitteln des Baessler-Instituts,* 5): 1–54.
Densmore, Frances.
1929 *Chippewa Customs.* Washington, D.C. (Smithsonian Institution, Bureau of American Ethnology, Bulletin 86).
Fonda, John H.
"Reminiscences of Wisconsin," *Wisconsin Historical Collections,* vol. 5, 276.
Hallowell, A. Irving.
1942 *The Role of Conjuring in Saulteaux Society.* Philadelphia (Publications of the Philadelphia Anthropological Society, 2).

BIBLIOGRAPHY

1960 "Ojibwa Ontology, Behavior, and World View," *Culture in History: Essays in Honor of Paul Radin*. New York, ed. Stanley Diamond, 19–52.

Helbig, Alethea K., ed.

1987 *Nanabozhoo Giver of Life*. Brighton, Michigan.

Henry, Alexander.

1809 *Travels and Adventures in Canada and the Indian Territories, between the years 1760 and 1776*. (Reprinted 1966, Ann Arbor, Michigan.)

Hickerson, Harold.

1962 *The Southwestern Chippewa: An Ethnohistorical Study*. Menasha, WI (American Anthropological Association, Memoir 92.)

Hoffman, Walter J.

1891 "The Medewiwin or 'Grand Medicine Society' of the Ojibwa," *Bureau of Ethnology, Seventh Annual Report, 1885–1886*. Washington, D.C.: 143–300.

Johnston, Basil.

1976 *Ojibway Heritage*. Toronto.

1982 *Ojibway Ceremonies*. (Republished 1990, Lincoln, Nebraska).

Jones, James A.

1830 *Traditions of the North American Indians*. London.

Jones, William.

1917,

1919 *Ojibwa Texts*. Leyden, New York, ed. Truman Michelson (Publications of the American Ethnological Society, 7, Parts 1,2) Leyden and N.Y.

Kidder, Homer Huntington.

1898a "Letter to A. Kidder," American Philosophical Society Library Archives, Philadelphia, Pa.

1898b "Two Local Indian Traditions," *The Mining Journal* (Marquette, Michigan, Jan. 1, 1898, 13).

Kinietz, W. Vernon.

1947 *Chippewa Village, the Story of Katikitegon*. Bloomfield Hills, Michigan.

Kohl, J. G.

1860 *Kitchi-Gami. Life Among The Lake Superior Ojibway*. trans. L.Wraxall, R. Neufang, U. Böcker (Reprinted 1985, St. Paul).

Lahoutan, Louis Armand de Lom d'Arcede.

1703 *Nouveaux voyages de Mr. le baron de Lahoutan dan l'Amerique septentrionale*. 2 vols. in l, The Hague.

1905 *New Voyages to North America by the Baron de Lahontan* [1703]. Reuben G. Thwaites ed. 2 vols. Chicago.

Laidlaw, George E.

1914–

1925 "Certain Ojibwa Myths" and "Ojibwa Myths and Tales," *Ontario Annual Archaeological Report*, 26: 77–79; 27: 71–90; 28: 84–92; 30: 74–110; 32: 66–85; 33: 84–99; 35: 34–80.

Landes, Ruth.

1968 *Ojibwa Religion and the Midéwiwin*. Madison.

Lévi-Strauss, Claude.

1985 *La potière jalouse*. Paris.

Bibliography

1988 *The Jealous Potter.* Chicago.

Maynard, Daniel P.

1990 "Marquette's Kawbawgams," in *Michigan History* 74, no. 2, pp. 36–39.

McKenney, Thomas L.

1827 *Sketches of a Tour to the Lakes, of the Character and Customs of the Chippeway Indians, and of Incidents Connected with the Treaty of Fond du Lac.* (Reprinted, 1959, Minneapolis.)

Morriseau, Norval.

1965 *Legends of My People,* ed. Selwyn Dewdney. Toronto.

Perrot, Nicolas.

1864 *Memoire sur les moeurs, coustumes et religion des sauvages de l'Ameique septentrionale* [1717]. Leipzig and Paris.

1911 "Memoire on the Manners, Customs, and Religion of the Savages of North America." in vol. 1 of *The Indian Tribes of the Upper Mississippi Valley and Region of the Great Lakes,* ed. Emma H. Blair. Cleveland.

Peters, Bernard C.

1984 "The Origin and Meaning of Chippewa Place Names Along the Lake Superior Shoreline Between Grand Island and Point Abbaye," *Michigan Academician* 14, 1, 234–251.

Polkinghorne, Donald E.

1988 *Narrative Knowing and the Human Sciences.* Albany, New York.

Radin, Paul.

1914 *Some Myths and Tales of the Ojibwa of Southeastern Ontario.* Ottawa. (Canada Department of Mines, Geological Survey, Museum Bulletin 2, Anthropological Series, 2).

Radin, Paul and Albert B. Reagan.

1928 "Ojibwa Myths and Tales," *Journal of American Folklore* 41: 61–146.

Ritzenthaler, Robert E. and Pat.

1970 *The Woodland Indians of the Western Great Lakes.* New York.

Rydholm, C. Fred.

1989 *Superior Heartland: A Backwoods History in Four Parts.* 2 vols. Marquette, Michigan.

Schoolcraft, Henry Rowe.

1848 *The Indian in His Wigwam or Characteristics of the Red Race of America.* New York.

1855 *Information, Respecting the History, Condition and Prospects of the Indian Tribes of the United States: Collected and Prepared under the Direction of the Bureau of Indian Affairs, per Act of Congress of March 3, 1847.* Philadelphia.

1856 *The Hiawatha Legends.* (Republished 1984, AuTrain, Michigan).

Skinner, Alanson.

1913 "Social Life and Ceremonial Bundles of the Menomini Indians," *Anthropological Papers of the American Museum of Natural History* XII, Pt. 1.

Skinner, Alanson and John V. Satterlee.

1915 "Folklore of the Menomini Indians," *Anthropological Papers of the American Museum of Natural History* XIII, Pt. 3.

BIBLIOGRAPHY

Thwaites, Reuben Gold, ed.

1896–

1901 *The Jesuit Relations and Allied Documents. Travels and Explorations of the Jesuit Missionaries in New France 1610–1791.* 73 vols. Cleveland.

Vecsey, Christopher.

1971 *Traditional Ojibwa Religion and Its Historical Changes.* Philadelphia.

1988 *Imagine Ourselves Richly, Mythic Narratives of North American Indians.* New York.

Warren, William W.

1852 *History of The Ojibway Nation* (Reprinted 1957, Minneapolis).

Williams, Mentor L., ed.

1956 *Schoolcraft's Indian Legends.* East Lansing, Michigan.

Williams, Ralph D.

1907 *The Honorable Peter White, A Biographical Sketch of the Lake Superior Iron Country.* Cleveland.

Titles in the Great Lakes Books Series

Freshwater Fury: Yarns and Reminiscences of the Greatest Storm in Inland Navigation, by Frank Barcus, 1986 (reprint)

Call It North Country: The Story of Upper Michigan, by John Bartlow Martin, 1986 (reprint)

The Land of the Crooked Tree, by U. P. Hedrick, 1986 (reprint)

Michigan Place Names, by Walter Romig, 1986 (reprint)

Luke Karamazov, by Conrad Hilberry, 1987

The Late, Great Lakes: An Environmental History, by William Ashworth, 1987 (reprint)

Great Pages of Michigan History from the Detroit Free Press, 1987

Waiting for the Morning Train: An American Boyhood, by Bruce Catton, 1987 (reprint)

Michigan Voices: Our State's History in the Words of the People Who Lived it, compiled and edited by Joe Grimm, 1987

Danny and the Boys, Being Some Legends of Hungry Hollow, by Robert Traver, 1987 (reprint)

Hanging On, or How to Get through a Depression and Enjoy Life, by Edmund G. Love, 1987 (reprint)

The Situation in Flushing, by Edmund G. Love, 1987 (reprint)

A Small Bequest, by Edmund G. Love, 1987 (reprint)

The Saginaw Paul Bunyan, by James Stevens, 1987 (reprint)

The Ambassador Bridge: A Monument to Progress, by Philip P. Mason, 1988

Let the Drum Beat: A History of the Detroit Light Guard, by Stanley D. Solvick, 1988

An Afternoon in Waterloo Park, by Gerald Dumas, 1988 (reprint)

Contemporary Michigan Poetry: Poems from the Third Coast, edited by Michael Delp, Conrad Hilberry, and Herbert Scott, 1988

Over the Graves of Horses, by Michael Delp, 1988

Wolf in Sheep's Clothing: The Search for a Child Killer, by Tommy McIntyre, 1988

Copper-Toed Boots, by Marguerite de Angeli, 1989 (reprint)

Detroit Images: Photographs of the Renaissance City, edited by John J. Bukowczyk and Douglas Aikenhead, with Peter Slavcheff, 1989

Hangdog Reef: Poems Sailing the Great Lakes, by Stephen Tudor, 1989

Detroit: City of Race and Class Violence, revised edition, by B. J. Widick, 1989

Deep Woods Frontier: A History of Logging in Northern Michigan, by Theodore J. Karamanski, 1989

Orvie, The Dictator of Dearborn, by David L. Good, 1989

Seasons of Grace: A History of the Catholic Archdiocese of Detroit, by Leslie Woodcock Tentler, 1990

The Pottery of John Foster: Form and Meaning, by Gordon and Elizabeth Orear, 1990

The Diary of Bishop Frederic Baraga: First Bishop of Marquette, Michigan, edited by Regis M. Walling and Rev. N. Daniel Rupp, 1990

Walnut Pickles and Watermelon Cake: A Century of Michigan Cooking, by Larry B. Massie and Priscilla Massie, 1990

The Making of Michigan, 1820–1860: A Pioneer Anthology, edited by Justin L. Kestenbaum, 1990

America's Favorite Homes: A Guide to Popular Early Twentieth-Century Homes, by Robert Schweitzer and Michael W. R. Davis, 1990

Beyond the Model T: The Other Ventures of Henry Ford, by Ford R. Bryan, 1990

Life after the Line, by Josie Kearns, 1990

Michigan Lumbertowns: Lumbermen and Laborers in Saginaw, Bay City, and Muskegon, 1870–1905, by Jeremy W. Kilar, 1990

Detroit Kids Catalog: The Hometown Tourist, by Ellyce Field, 1990

Waiting for the News, by Leo Litwak, 1990 (reprint)

Detroit Perspectives, edited by Wilma Wood Henrickson, 1991

Life on the Great Lakes: A Wheelsman's Story, by Fred W. Dutton, edited by William Donohue Ellis, 1991

Copper Country Journal: The Diary of Schoolmaster Henry Hobart, 1863–1864, by Henry Hobart, edited by Philip P. Mason, 1991

John Jacob Astor: Business and Finance in the Early Republic, by John Denis Haeger, 1991

Survival and Regeneration: Detroit's American Indian Community, by Edmund J. Danziger, Jr., 1991

Steamboats and Sailors of the Great Lakes, by Mark L. Thompson, 1991

Cobb Would Have Caught It: The Golden Years of Baseball in Detroit, by Richard Bak, 1991

Michigan in Literature, by Clarence Andrews, 1992

Under the Influence of Water: Poems, Essays, and Stories, by Michael Delp, 1992

The Country Kitchen, by Della T. Lutes, 1992 (reprint)

The Making of a Mining District: Keweenaw Native Copper 1500–1870, by David J. Krause, 1992

Kids Catalog of Michigan Adventures, by Ellyce Field, 1993

Henry's Lieutenants, by Ford R. Bryan, 1993

Historic Highway Bridges of Michigan, by Charles K. Hyde, 1993

Lake Erie and Lake St. Clair Handbook, by Stanley J. Bolsenga and Charles E. Herndendorf, 1993

Queen of the Lakes, by Mark Thompson, 1994

Iron Fleet: The Great Lakes in World War II, by George J. Joachim, 1994

Turkey Stearnes and the Detroit Stars: The Negro Leagues in Detroit, 1919–1933, by Richard Bak, 1994

Pontiac and the Indian Uprising, by Howard H. Peckham, 1994 (reprint)

Charting the Inland Seas: A History of the U.S. Lake Survey, by Arthur M. Woodford, 1994 (reprint)

Ojibwa Narratives of Charles and Charlotte Kawbawgam and Jacques LePique, 1893–1895. Recorded with Notes by Homer H. Kidder, edited by Arthur P. Bourgeois, 1994, Co-published with the Marquette County Historical Society